"Toby Landesman....has given a voice to the great resources that Jewish life has to offer those in need. As a rabbi, I value the marvelous tool she has given me through which I can learn and with which I can help others. I thank her for making the wisdom of the ages available to a general readership."

Rabbi Mark Dratch
Rabbinical Council of A

D1329399

"[*You Are Not Alone* is] a comprehensive and compelling resource for battered women who want to heal in a Jewish spiritual context. Every rabbi, therapist, educator, and Jewish community professional should have this on their bookshelf!"

Naomi Tucker, Co-founder and Executive Director
Shalom Bayit (Bay Area Jewish Women Working
to End Domestic Violence)
San Francisco, CA

"When a victim of abuse seeks support from a rabbi or other Jewish leader, the most powerful help that any of us can offer is, of course, the power of our tradition and the connection that this provides with God. With the publication of this book, I have a new, compassionate resource, giving abuse survivors a way to be reunited with the unconditional support and love of Judaism."

Rabbi Julie S. Schwartz
Temple Emanu-El
Atlanta, GA

"This powerful, life-changing book by Toby Landesman puts an end to the myth that abuse doesn't happen in Jewish homes. It does, and as Landesman proves so compellingly, there is hope, there is healing, there is a way out of the pain. But before that healing can happen, Jews in positions of power – those allocating the resources and speaking from our pulpits – have to wake up to the reality that Jews are hurting other Jews. *You Are Not Alone* weaves the beautiful, haunting, courageous voices of abuse survivors with crucial information on what victims, families, community members, and rabbis can do to acknowledge, heal, and stop family violence. This rich, vital resource is one no congregation can afford to be without. Go out and buy it today."

Laura Davis
Author, I Thought We'd Never Speak Again
Co-author, The Courage to Heal

"*You Are Not Alone: Solace and Inspiration for Domestic Violence Survivors Based on Jewish Wisdom* aptly fulfills the promise of its title. It helps those experiencing abuse to see that they are not alone and that abuse is not their fault, and it gives them resources to understand their feelings, to find help, to create safety for themselves and their children, and to begin again, all with informative and clear prose and emotionally compelling poetry. I only hope that it gets into the hands of the many who need it so that it can bring the healing and new life they deserve."

Rabbi Elliot Dorff
Professor of Philosophy, University of Judaism
Author, Love Your Neighbor and Yourself: A Jewish
Approach to Modern Personal Ethics

You Are Not Alone

Solace and Inspiration for
Domestic Violence Survivors
Based on Jewish Wisdom

by Toby Landesman

PREFACE BY RABBI MARK DRATCH

FaithTrust

INSTITUTE

Working together to end
sexual & domestic violence

2400 N. 45th Street, Suite 10
Seattle, WA 98103
www.faithtrustinstitute.org

You Are Not Alone: Solace and Inspiration for Domestic Violence
Survivors Based on Jewish Wisdom

Toby Landesman

FaithTrust Institute
2400 N. 45th Street, Suite 10
Seattle, WA 98103
www.faithtrustinstitute.org

Unless otherwise noted, all English translations of Biblical texts are from
JPS Hebrew-English TANAKH (2nd edition) (Philadelphia: The Jewish Publication
Society, 1999).

Cover photograph and photograph on page 37 by Toby Landesman, © Toby
Landesman. Used with permission.

Design by Moonlight Design

ISBN 0-9745189-1-3

Printed in the United States of America

Permissions/Credits

The publisher sincerely thanks the following sources for their permission to reprint previously published material. We apologize for any inadvertent errors or omissions on our part, and will correct them in future editions. This page constitutes an extension of the copyright page.

Rabbi David R. Blumenthal: Excerpt from "Liturgies of Anger," *Cross Currents*, Vol. 52, No. 2 (Summer 2002). Reprinted by permission of Rabbi David R. Blumenthal.

Rabbi Elliot Dorff: Excerpt from "Jewish Law and Tradition," in *Shine the Light: Sexual Abuse and Healing in the Jewish Community* by Rachel Lev (Boston: Northeastern University Press, 2003). Reprinted by permission of Rabbi Elliot Dorff.

Marcia Falk: The passages by Marcia Falk are excerpted from *The Book of Blessings: New Jewish Prayers for Daily Life, the Sabbath, and the New Moon Festival* (Harper, 1996; Beacon, 1999). Copyright © 1996 by Marcia Lee Falk. Reprinted by permission of Marcia Falk.

The Haworth Press, Inc.: Excerpt from "Forgiveness and the Jewish High Holy Days," by Marcia Cohn Spiegel, in *Forgiveness and Abuse: Jewish and Christian Reflections* © 2002, The Haworth Press, Binghamton, New York. Reprinted by permission of The Haworth Press, Inc.

Jewish Lights Publishing: Excerpt from *Sacred Intentions: Daily Inspiration to Strengthen the Spirit, Based on Jewish Wisdom* © 1999 Rabbi Kerry M. Olitzky and Rabbi Lori Forman (Woodstock, VT: Jewish Lights Publishing). Permission granted by Jewish Lights Publishing, P.O. Box 237, Woodstock, VT 05091 www.jewishlights.com.

to my mother, whose delight and awe in the little and big things in life continue to inspire me

– Toby Landesman

FaithTrust Institute acknowledges our deep gratitude to Rabbi Julie R. Spitzer (z"l) for her pioneering work on domestic violence in Jewish communities.
May her memory be for a blessing.

Table of Contents

Acknowledgments

I feel deeply honored and grateful for the generosity of so many who gave of their time, knowledge and materials to help create this book. My floor is strewn with borrowed books, my computer with shared thoughts and my heart with the compassion of those who walk this journey for peace and safety in Jewish lives.

Thanks especially to:

Marcia Cohn Spiegel, Hadassah Goodman, Fayge Siegal, Debby Leibenstein, Sherry Berliner Dimarsky and Julia Atkinson for their friendship, support and faith in me.

Wendy Lipshutz, Barbara Siegel, Rabbi Mark Dratch, Rabbi Elliot Dorff, Rabbi Dr. Jerry Lob, Leigh Nachman Hofheimer, Naomi Tucker and Toby Myers for their help with the development of this resource and their ongoing work to end violence in people's lives.

And, the survivors for sharing their experience, strength and hope.

Working with Jean Anton of FaithTrust Institute has been a delight. A great editor and arbiter of the comma, she unfailingly demonstrates what it means to honor and work in partnership. Rabbi Cindy G. Enger provided support, knowledge, wisdom and insights.

For their generous sharing of time and knowledge, special thanks are extended to the following reviewers of this book:

Connie Burk, The Northwest Network of Bisexual, Trans, Lesbian, and Gay Survivors of Abuse (Seattle)

Rabbi Elliot Dorff, University of Judaism

Rabbi Mark Dratch, Rabbinical Council of America

Rabbi Dayle A. Friedman, Hiddur: The Center for Aging and Judaism (Wyncote, PA)

Leigh Nachman Hofheimer, Washington State Coalition Against Domestic Violence

Leslie Landis, Mayor's Office on Domestic Violence (Chicago)

Wendy Lipshutz, Shalom Bayit Program, Jewish Family & Career Services (Atlanta)

Toby Myers, longtime worker in Texas battered women's movement

Rabbi Julie S. Schwartz, Temple Emanu-El (Atlanta)

Barbara Siegel, SHALVA (Chicago)

Naomi Tucker, Shalom Bayit (Bay Area Women Working to End Domestic Violence) (San Francisco)

Preface

"Avadim hayyinu" – We were slaves in Egypt (Deuteronomy 6:21).
Victimized by the unbridled power and oppressive cruelty of their
taskmasters, our ancestors lived from day to day, minute to minute, bent
under their burdens, barely able to see beyond their mud-encrusted feet.
And then God called to Moses from a burning bush with the possibility of
hope and the promise of a redeemed future. "And God said, 'I have surely
seen the affliction of my people who are in Egypt, and have heard their cry
because of their taskmasters; for I know their sorrows.'" (Exodus 3:7).

Even before one chain was cut or one lash was thwarted, while still
confined in the house of bondage, the rays of hope and the promise of a
new day began to heal their broken bodies, lift their crushed spirits and
heal their futile dreams. How? Because they learned that someone
cared. Because they learned that this is not how life had to be. Because
they dared to imagine a different future.

This book, *You Are Not Alone: Solace and Inspiration for Domestic
Violence Survivors Based on Jewish Wisdom*, is an important resource for
survivors, for future survivors, and for the Jewish community at large. If
you are a survivor or future survivor, you will find words of wisdom and
comfort, words of hope and solace. You will find practical information to
help you understand your situation and to learn about some of your
options and the resources available. If you are a concerned friend or
rabbi, you will gain insight and understanding, and be helped in your
desire to help others.

In addition to all of this, *You Are Not Alone* is an act of *teshuvah*, of
contrition and repentance for the Jewish community, which for too many
years has been in a state of denial regarding the problem of domestic

violence and has been guilty of silence. For many reasons, we have not exercised one of the strongest muscles in the human body, our jaw muscles, to speak out against violence, to acknowledge the pain and suffering of our wives, mothers, sisters, and daughters, and to offer the words necessary to reclaim *shalom bayit*, peaceful and harmonious domestic relations.

This silence is anathema to Jewish values, a tradition that is rich in compassion and empathy. The Talmud (*Yevamot 79a*) notes that as a people, we are distinguished by three traits: mercy, modesty and benevolence. When these traits are absent, Jewish law instructs us to evaluate whether we are meeting our basic obligations as Jews.

Sure, we'd like to think that it doesn't happen to us, but reality teaches us otherwise. Try telling a battered woman that her Jewish husband didn't hit her or telling someone who is subjected to ridicule and insults that such things don't happen in Jewish marriages. Not all Jews are merciful, modest and benevolent. We cannot let our illusions enable someone else's nightmares. We cannot fail to respond to those who call for our help. We can no longer respond with the deafening silence of indifference and denial. This would be a *Chillul Hashem* (desecration of God's Name) of massive proportions. Judaism demands justice and commands us to help those in need. We must provide for the healing of survivors and the accountability of abusers.

For many who live their lives within a Jewish context, the way toward healing and wholeness is within a Jewish context as well. Jewish responses do not replace counseling, social service support, or the legal system, but they can color the attitudes, approaches and choices we make, and they can certainly be a source of great hope and inspiration. Some of those who read this book may live as Orthodox Jews, strictly according to the dictates of Halacha (Jewish law); others may identify and practice as Reform, Conservative, Reconstructionist, Renewal or Humanistic Jews. Some others may identify as Jewish by reason of family or upbringing or culture. Regardless of your perspective, there is much in your Jewish legacy and traditions that can serve as a source of help and healing. There is much in this book that is for you.

Toby Landesman has done a formidable job in amassing many sources from the broad spectrum of Jewish expression, both traditional and contemporary. In her sensitive, empathic and accessible style, she has given a voice to the great resources that Jewish life has to offer those in need. She has opened the door of Jewish tradition to all – those who are committed and actively Jewish as well as those who may feel alienated, alone and estranged from our community. As a rabbi, I value the marvelous tool she has given me through which I can learn and with which I can help others. I thank her for making the wisdom of the ages available to a general readership. And as a member of the domestic violence community, I know how great this contribution is for the many Jewish victims and the professionals who support them.

This book is published under the auspices of FaithTrust Institute, a unique and invaluable resource for all religious communities. The product of the dream of a great pioneer, Rev. Dr. Marie M. Fortune, and its many religious, professional and lay supporters, FaithTrust Institute has been in the vanguard of the issue of domestic violence in faith communities. It has held each of us responsible for those in our communities who are suffering, and for the suffering that is too often caused within our communities. My personal involvement, both as a member of its Jewish Advisory Committee and as a contributor to some of its invaluable publications, is among my proudest achievements as a rabbi. Many thanks as well to Rev. Kathryn Jans, Executive Director; Rabbi Cindy G. Enger, Director of the Jewish Program; and Jean Anton, Resource Director, for her grace and diligence.

Among the many interesting figures on my wife's family tree is a simple Polish rabbi of the eighteenth century known as the "*Hoicher*," the Yiddish word for "the tall one." Now, although there are many prominent and distinguished rabbis of great stature in this lineage, none of them is known for his physical height. As a matter of fact, standing 6'2", I tower over them all. So why was this Rabbi Yehoshua called "the tall one?" You see, family legend has it that all week long, he walked stooped over, bent by the burdens and angst of his difficult life. But on Shabbat, the Holy Sabbath, as he left the burdens of the workdays behind him, his back straightened, his shoulders pulled back, his head was held high. On the holy, pure Day of Rest, he stood tall. To survivors of abuse I say, "The Sabbath is coming! Peace, rest, and safety in the embrace of your community."

Rabbi Mark Dratch

| Introduction

This book is for all members of the Jewish community who seek spiritual comfort and guidance as you confront domestic violence or abuse in an intimate relationship. Our message to you is, "You are not alone."

Domestic violence occurs within all streams of Judaism: Conservative, Orthodox, Reconstructionist, Reform, Renewal and among Jews who are unaffiliated or who do not identify with any particular Movement. It happens in Jewish relationships across all socio-economic, religious and political lines and without regard for geographic boundaries. It occurs in heterosexual and same-gender relationships. It occurs in both adult and teen relationships. While both men and women can be abusive, it is important to emphasize that 85% of partner abuse is committed by men against women.[1] You are not alone.

Although this resource does not fully reflect the experience of same-gender abuse (particularly as the tactics are more complex and the response from the community and societal institutions is different), many of the readings that offer spiritual support may still apply and be helpful. You are not alone.

Jewish and secular sources from the Bible to modern times give proof of the existence of abuse within Jewish families and relationships.

> It is not an enemy who reviles me – I could bear that;
> …but it is you, my equal, my companion, my friend.
> *Psalm 55:13-14*[2]

Within these pages, Jewish text and tradition and the voices of survivors offer ways to heal, to gain strength, to move forward. In this book, the words of survivors are identified by gray background shading. These quotes are from survivors who shared their stories with domestic violence advocates or directly with the author. Some quotes are based on an individual's experience, while others are composites. All are true. Details were changed only to protect identity.

As we turn to Judaism for comfort, we also acknowledge that neither the Jewish tradition nor its texts and teachers have uniformly condemned domestic violence; some have even condoned hitting and disciplining one's wife.[3] While this is a source of pain, there is much within Jewish tradition that can be used to heal. Because of the community's silence and misinformation about abuse, survivors of domestic violence sometimes say they didn't fully realize what was happening to them for a long time. When our communities perpetuate abuse by not naming abusive patterns openly and not holding abusers accountable, victims of abuse cannot accurately name the actions of their partners as being abusive.

While this is neither a self-help book nor a domestic violence guide, because of the serious, potentially lethal, consequences of domestic violence, we have included basic information on the dynamics of domestic violence. The resources and bibliography sections offer ways to learn more, as well as places to go for help.

To be abused by your partner or spouse is terrifying and bewildering. Whether you leave or stay, you may feel judged and abandoned by a culture and community that doesn't believe you, doesn't hold your abuser accountable, sometimes blames you, and doesn't provide the practical, emotional and spiritual resources you need. You may have discovered that leaving doesn't necessarily assure the end of danger, that sometimes it even gets worse, that children can get caught in the middle. You are not alone.

We hope, with this resource, to offer you support and comfort on your journey toward safety and healing. What comforts or inspires can differ from person to person and day to day. Our intention is to provide solace and inspiration in ways that reflect a diversity of Jewish thought and practice. All of this is offered with the deepest respect for each individual's path. If the language or content in any given section doesn't work for you, consider looking beneath the language to the spiritual meaning, changing the language, or skipping to other sections.

Psalms (*Tehillim*) have been a source of comfort for many centuries. At the same time, some content in psalms can be disturbing or unsettling. Attempts have been made to honor tradition while respecting the needs of individuals to feel safe while talking to God. Within this book, excerpts from psalms were selected based on these considerations. Be aware of this if you choose to look outside this book at the entire psalm from which a selection was made. As in the rest of life, something beautiful can be found before, after, or even within, something jarring. The anguish and suffering portrayed in a number of psalms confirms our message: you are not alone.

Within the context of a world in which international and domestic terrorism are far too common, Rabbi Simkha Y. Weintraub, C.S.W., wrote about Jewish spiritual resources to strengthen our spirit. His words reflect the intent, the *kavannah*, of this book. "The goal is *not* to neatly package or explain away the inexplicable, nor to deny pain or silence anger, nor to insist on anyone 'getting over it already.' It is, rather, to enable people to relate to one another, to the broader community, and to an age-old tradition in light of both the horrors and the *hessed* (lovingkindness) around us, perhaps to experience some care and transcendence, a sense of hope and possibility."[4]

Judaism expects us to keep ourselves and each other safe (*pikuach nefesh*: to save a life, including one's own). When there is danger, we must first and foremost do what we can to be safe. Information on safety planning and resources are included in the back of the book.

How can you use this book? Whenever possible, find a quiet time and place for yourself. Select a section from the table of contents or browse through and see what catches your eye. Take a breath, evoke the presence of God (whatever that means for you), and slowly recite the psalms, prayers or stories. Hold the words sweetly on your tongue and softly in your heart. Feel the care and compassion of God. Feel the care and compassion of each and all of us who pray and work with you to bring safety and tranquility to every Jewish home. You are not alone. Shalom.

2 How Do I Know if I am Being Abused?

ASK YOURSELF:

○ Does my partner frequently criticize me?

○ Do I feel I'm living a lie when I say our relationship is fine?

○ Is my partner overly jealous of my relationships with family, friends, co-workers?

○ Do I feel like I'm walking on eggshells in my home?

○ Am I or my children afraid/worried when my partner walks through the door?

○ Do I spend a lot of time trying to read my partner's moods and doing things to lessen the chance of another argument or fight?

○ Does my partner insist on making the rules? On controlling decision-making? On being "right?"

○ Does my partner do things that leave me feeling humiliated?

○ Does my partner blame me for his/her outbursts saying, "If only you did/didn't _____, I wouldn't get so upset?"

○ Does my partner threaten to hurt him/herself or me if I leave the relationship?

○ Does my partner threaten to take the children away if he/she thinks I am leaving the relationship?

○ Am I ever afraid that I won't live another day?

○ Do I ever question that I am physically and emotionally safe in this relationship?

If your answer to any of these is yes –
you could be in a situation of domestic violence.

WHAT IS DOMESTIC VIOLENCE?

Domestic violence is a pattern of abuse and/or coercion by which one
person controls and manipulates another in an intimate/romantic
relationship. Tactics of abuse can be physical, sexual, emotional,
economic and spiritual. Some behaviors, like a slap, are obvious; others,
like "you must pick up the phone by the third ring, or else" – rules
established by the abuser, may be more subtle. Domestic violence is not
an isolated, individual event. People sometimes use other terms when
discussing domestic violence, including intimate partner violence
and battering.

How hard it can be to acknowledge that these words and definitions
describe what is happening to you. "But," you say, "it doesn't happen all
the time." Attacks don't happen 24 hours a day, 7 days a week. Some
days will be free from abuse. There will even be "good" days. The key
is whether the attacks return and whether there is a pattern of coercion in
your relationship. The descriptions in the categories below may help
you decide if this is happening to you.

Many people ask, "But, who would do such things?"

> Abuse is generally committed by people who appear
> normal in every other domain of their lives. Abusive
> behavior is not about anger and frustration. It is a desire
> to have power and control. The abuser will often
> describe it as anger. It isn't. Domestic violence is not a
> crime of passion. It's not bad temper. Domestic violence
> is a crime of possession – a sense of entitlement –
> thinking you own another person, that you can use any
> means you want.
>
> *Alana Bowman*[5]

IT'S DANGEROUS

Domestic violence is always potentially deadly. When someone's intent is to control, verbal assaults can become physical. Each of us has the right to be safe. If you are being physically hurt, or belittled, or demeaned, or if you feel afraid in your relationship, please talk with someone you trust – an advocate at a domestic violence program, a therapist, a rabbi. Be sure the person you choose has experience with domestic violence situations.

TACTICS OF ABUSE

PHYSICAL ABUSE

Physical abuse can include hitting, kicking, punching, pinching, burning, the use of weapons or objects, biting or pushing. If you are being deprived of food, sleep, or medication, or are being restrained in one place, this is also physical abuse.

He terrorized me and the kids – screaming and yelling, swearing. He even hit the kids at times, and tried to hit me. Since he didn't hurt me much physically, I didn't think of myself as being abused. I didn't think anyone would understand what it meant to live at the mercy of his whims and moods, his anger...I was so scared.[6]

My partner pushed me against the wall and slid a thumb in my jugular saying, "One way or another, you're going to shut up and listen."

He told me it was only a matter of time before he killed me. I believed him when he said, "If I can't have you, no one can."

SEXUAL ABUSE

Any forced or unwanted sexual contact, sexual humiliation, or mutilation of the sexual organs or breasts is sexual abuse. Sexual abuse also includes situations in which you agree to have sex because you are afraid of how your partner might respond if you refuse.

My husband raped me in our marital bed.

He checks my underpants when he comes home to make sure I haven't been sexually involved with someone else.

My husband watches pornography on the Internet on the computer in our bedroom most nights before we go to bed. He turns up the sound, sits on the edge of the bed and masturbates. He won't let me leave the room.

My partner touches me whether or not I want to be touched. Saying "no" or "stop" or "don't" makes no difference. It is especially awful when we're in public. I feel exposed, ashamed. Then later, if I've gone along, I'm called a slut. If I didn't, I'm "frigid."

INTIMIDATION

Intimidation can come in physical or verbal forms, including threats of violence, violence against others including pets, destruction of property, harassment at work, and extended periods of silence. Threatening to harm the children and/or harming them, manipulating the children, threatening to abduct them and/or using visitation to harass you are examples of intimidation.

For years he would threaten me, back me in a corner and raise his hands, but he never touched me. He'd do it with the most wicked, rageful look on his face. I live in constant fear, always humiliated. The worst part about the whole thing is that he does not see this as a problem. He says the problem is with me. He says I don't understand him and he needs my love.

My partner abused me and our children with silence. If we weren't sufficiently contrite, if we didn't wish 'Good morning' just the right way, the silence fell. We never knew what the right way was. All we knew is that when the silence fell, we must have done it wrong.

Barry would hit our son in front of me. If I tried to intervene he'd hit him harder. Barry knew he could get me more upset by hurting our son than hitting me.

Jerry undermines my authority with the kids. It's things like, "Oh, your mother said you have to do your homework? You don't. Let's go out and have a good time. Your mother worries too much. She is so sensitive." Then later when I ask the kids how their homework is going they say, "Dad says we don't have to do this. You're crazy."

Immigrant/refugee women who are being battered may face unique challenges.

> *He says things that scare me. Sometimes he tells me that he will make bad things happen to me. Sometimes he says he will kill himself if I do not obey him. He said this in front of our son! He tells me I am crazy. He says he will get a big and expensive American lawyer to make sure I never see my child again. My English is not so good. I do not know what to do. He has money. He has relatives. I am all alone in this country.*

> *My husband told me he'd have me deported and keep our children here if I didn't do exactly what he said. I believed him. I'd seen it happen to others.[7]*

OTHER FORMS OF INTIMIDATION

If you are being followed, your property is being destroyed, or your partner is leaving unwanted notes or constantly calling you, this is intimidation.

Notes on a car, constant phone calls, and wanting to be alone with you can sound like the romantic stage of a relationship. How can we distinguish love and passion from abuse? The issue is control. Gavin de Becker, expert on the prediction and management of violence, suggests asking yourself: When you say, "Don't do that. I don't like it," does the person listen and stop doing it? Can s/he be influenced? De Becker also encourages you to trust your intuition, your sense that something is wrong, that something is "off."[8]

EMOTIONAL ABUSE

How complicated and confusing this form of coercive control is. Not as overt as a push, shove or slap, emotional abuse eats away at your confidence, your sense of self. Threats of harm to you or others, of "taking the kids," of not paying for the children's education or health care, can be just as effective as physical violence in keeping you feeling trapped. Emotional abuse can be active or passive. The silent treatment is an example of passive emotional abuse. Being belittled, demeaned or kept from participating in major decisions are also forms of emotional abuse.

Regularly being told, *"You're stupid, fat, ugly, unlovable,"* constitutes emotional abuse. Smirks, eye rolls, stern looks and long silences that last days or weeks or months without ever a hint of what "terrible" thing you've done are examples of emotional abuse. When all affection and warmth are withdrawn and you sit and ponder what you did, when you are bossed around as if you are a prisoner or slave, when you are treated like property rather than a human being, you are being emotionally abused.

> Emotional abuse is an insidious way of establishing control over another person. The methods of establishing control over another person are based upon the systematic, repetitive infliction of psychological trauma...It is not necessary to use violence often to keep the victim in a constant state of fear.
>
> *Judith Lewis Herman, M.D.[9]*

The psychological impact of emotional abuse can be as devastating as other forms of abuse.

If you are being demeaned or belittled, it's just as bad as being hit.[10]

SPIRITUAL ABUSE

ASK YOURSELF:

- ○ Does my partner obstruct me or the children from going to our own place of worship?

- ○ Does my partner put down my religious or spiritual beliefs?

- ○ Have I or the children been pressured or coerced to go to the place of worship my partner chooses?

- ○ Has my partner forced me or the children to eat or drink things prohibited by my beliefs?

- ○ Has my partner told me that God would not help me?

- ○ Has my partner told me that s/he was my God?

ISOLATION

Isolation occurs when you are denied access to 1) basic means of communication, 2) family and friends, 3) phones or cars, 4) a private life, 5) health care, 6) spiritual or cultural community.

Jay would say, "Don't call your mother. I don't like your friends. If you love me you'll stop seeing them." It became easier to cut these people out of my life than to try to sneak around or risk the explosions that came if it became known that I, God forbid, had lunch with my mother.

My partner checked the odometer on the car every night, then checked it with where I said I went that day. I did less and less driving. Eventually, it became easier to not go anywhere.

Sandy won't let me go to the mikveh anymore.

My husband disconnects our only phone and puts it in the trunk of his car every morning. He locks me in the basement before he leaves home.

My husband was impossible, but so so so smooth. I didn't realize until years later how he'd isolated me from everyone. First, he moved me and the kids out of town, away from my family and friends, away from my whole life. Then he wouldn't let me keep in touch with them. I thought I had it lucky. When he was good he was so very good. I kept accepting his apologies and telling myself things would get better. He was my husband and my children's father, and I was to keep the peace, keep the family together. It didn't work. Things got worse.

ECONOMIC ABUSE

As in all areas of a couple's life, there are many ways to make decisions about handling finances. It is important for all couples to discuss and negotiate how decisions will be made and re-negotiated. Economic abuse is evident when there is no discussion, no agreement between the couple, but where one person in the couple sets the rules. Controlling rules can include keeping you from getting a job, hiding family assets or information about them, denying access to money and/or controlling access to money, or forcing you to account for every penny spent.

> *I have no access to cash. I have to buy everything with a credit card. My partner monitors everywhere I go and everything I do by tracing where I spend money. I can't buy a pack of gum. What store would take a credit card for a pack of gum?*

> *My husband says, "Why do you need a checkbook? Don't I give you everything you need?"*

> *Last night he shouted, "If you don't do what I say, I'm pulling the kids out of the private school and telling them it's your fault."*

Controlling rules can also include insisting you work and run the house while your partner refuses to work, incurs debt and/or gambles.

These real examples demonstrate abuse – actions that attempt to control you and that frighten, disempower, humiliate, shame and/or isolate you.

REMEMBER, IT'S ON PURPOSE

People who abuse do so intentionally. They may say they didn't mean it. They may say they couldn't help themselves. They may say you caused it. The bottom line is that people who abuse want to control, intend to get their way and believe it is their right to do so. They are wrong.

3 What Judaism Says About Abuse

"Haray At M'kudeshet Li…" …the opening words of the
Jewish wedding vow, are recited by a groom to his bride.
Embedded in that vow is the root word *kadosh*, holy,
sacred, unique, set apart. As the groom and bride make
their declarations to one another, they are naming the
other as holy, as sacred, as unique. To make such a vow is
to declare before God and those assembled that your
beloved is created in the Divine image, and as such, has a
bit of *ruach Elohim*, a bit of the Divine spirit, as part of
every cell. Therefore, to cause harm to one's beloved is
not only to wrong another human being. It is tantamount
to wrong God.

Rabbi Julie R. Spitzer [11]

Anything which impinges on the dignity of another person
is considered abuse, and is a violation of Torah ethics.

Rabbi Abraham Twerski [12]

It's important we say out loud that morally it isn't okay
to physically, emotionally, spiritually or sexually abuse
or harm another. This is not the way a Jew should live.
We need to make a moral statement Jewishly speaking.

Sherry Berliner Dimarsky [13]

...the Rabbis took the notion of the integrity of the individual so far as to say that those who slander others (and certainly those who cause them physical injury) are as though they had denied the existence of God. (Jerusalem Talmud, Pe'ah 1:1)   Conversely, Rabbi Eliezer said, "Let your fellow's honor be as dear to you as your own." (M. Avot 2:15)

Rabbi Elliot Dorff [14]

If *Halachah* cannot protect a victim it is not [the correct interpretation of] *Halachah*.

Rabbi Mark Dratch [15]

MYTHS AND TRUTHS

Myths and contradictions exist within our Jewish communities about abuse:

❍ The myth that Jews don't abuse their partners, children or elders.

> But it is happening, right here in our midst. And sometimes the abusers are people we know and love... Often women will tell me, "he's such a *macher* in the community... no one will believe me."
>
> *Naomi Tucker* [16]

Within early Jewish texts as well as today's newspapers, one can find stories of murder, abuse, rape and incest in Jewish relationships.

❍ The myth that maintaining *shalom bayit* is entirely up to the woman of the house and that *shalom bayit* means keeping the family together even when domestic violence is present.

> For centuries, *shalom bayit*, household harmony, has been the hallmark of Jewish homes. It has been one of the few *mitzvot* accorded primarily to women. But it has also become a prison for many of those same women. "So he beats you once a month? That's only twelve times a year. How bad could that be? Your responsibility is to make *shalom bayit*. Go home to your husband. You can make it better." This is the advice given to one woman who was brave enough to seek help from her rabbi a few years ago.
>
> *Rabbi Julie R. Spitzer* [17]

○ The myth that it is a *Hillul Hashem*, a desecration of God, if you speak of being abused and that speaking about being abused is *lashon hara*, evil gossip.

Rabbi Mark Dratch reminds us that telling about abuse is not a desecration of God (*Hillul Hashem*) but an honoring of God (*Kiddush Hashem*). [18]

> While we are reminded against defaming someone, at the very same time the warning against *lashon hara* is not an excuse to avoid action if injustice is taking place around us. We have to be careful that the prohibition against *lashon hara* actually protects victims, rather than inadvertently silencing them.
>
> *Naomi Tucker* [19]

While rabbinic texts and teachings reveal contradictory views on domestic violence, [20] integral to Judaism is the honoring of life, including the imperative of *pikuach nefesh* – saving a life, including one's own.

ON RESPECT

Reverence for God is shown in our reverence for human beings...Human life is holy, holier even than the Scrolls of the Torah.

Rabbi Abraham Joshua Heschel [21]

Judaism doesn't condone violence. It doesn't say it's good to suffer. [As one rabbi said,] "The Torah teaches the importance of respecting people, maintaining a healthy relationship with God and one's fellow man. It isn't a means to exploit or put people in chains."

Rachel Lev [22]

ON VERBAL ABUSE

Verbal abuse violates not only the relationship among
the human beings involved, but also that between the
individual and God, for God commands us not to
oppress others. One honors God and the Jewish people
(*Kiddush Hashem*) when one honors others; conversely,
one dishonors God and desecrates God's people (*Hillul
Hashem*) when one verbally abuses a human being
created in the divine image.

Rabbi Elliot Dorff [23]

Do not go about as a slanderer among your kinspeople.

Leviticus 19:16 [24]

Shaming another in public is like shedding blood.

Talmud:Baba Metzia, 58b

IT'S A SHAME – A SHANDA

Being abused and victimized is not the *shanda*. Victimizing is the
shanda. Abusing is the *shanda*.

To all those who have been hurt or humiliated by your partner: know that you do not deserve this. No one has the right to tell you that you are worthless; your worth comes from God. Regardless of what anyone says about you, you are worthy: because you are created in the image of God. No one has the right to control you: you are a born equal; it is your God-given right to be treated with respect, including and especially by your partner. It is not your job to single-handedly defend *shalom bayit*, or peace in your home.

Naomi Tucker [25]

Community silence and denial are the *shanda*. Each community must take a stand for peace and tranquility in Jewish lives.

COMMUNITIES MUST TAKE A STAND

The Torah demands that we seek justice, that we love our neighbors as ourselves.[26] Individuals and organizations within a community have a responsibility to each other.

> As Jews we know that if one of us is enslaved or endangered, none of us is free. Our responsibility is to promote the end of abuse, to prevent future abuse, and to give people the skills and resources to help themselves and each other.
>
> *Kehilla Community Synagogue: Policy Guidelines on the Prevention of and Response to Abuse*[27]

> When you feel part of a community you want to take care of people in that community. When somebody is in pain or hurting or has been wronged you know it's important to step up to the plate and help that person. Or, when somebody has done something wrong you support sanctioning that person. Being part of a community means both being there for somebody who is in need and taking a stand when somebody is an actor of violence or violation. Members of a community don't turn their backs.
>
> *Esta Soler*[28]

We are exhorted by the Psalmist, "Seek peace and pursue it." We must consider not only peace among nations, not only peace between neighbors, but *shalom bayit*, peace in the household as well. *Shalom bayit*: We must recognize that not every household is one of peace and harmony, that violence exists in the Jewish community as much as it exists in the general population. That the end to such violence is expedited by awareness of the signs of a troubled home, and obligating ourselves not to turn away or pretend the problem doesn't exist. *Shalom bayit* must be held up as an ideal – not as a trap, but as a release. Keeping peace in the home is not a reason to stay in an abusive situation. It is a reason to <u>leave</u> one. Violence is cyclical, and it rarely gets better or goes away over time. Breaking the cycle of violence can help end it.

Rabbi Julie R. Spitzer [29]

4 Why is This Happening to Me?

> *He says it's my fault. If only I were a better wife, then he wouldn't get so upset. I do make mistakes. Maybe it is my fault.*

Neverekh et mekor hahayyim shebara et tzurot hahayyim leminei-hen, ve'et kulanu shelemim, gam im lo mushlamim.
Let us bless the Source of life in its infinite variety, that creates all of us whole, none of us perfect.

Judith Glass [30]

When you love someone, you are initially shocked and often confused by hurtful behavior. You try to tell yourself your loved one didn't mean it, that it won't happen again. You push it out of your mind. As it continues to happen, you keep looking for reasons to explain how what you've done made this happen – believing, hoping that you can then do something to make it stop. None of us can control another person's actions. Being human, forgetting things, being imperfect, making mistakes, whether small or huge, does not make someone else's abuse of you your fault. Violence and abuse are never your fault. No one deserves to be abused.

No matter what you have done or failed to do – no matter how big or small – you do not deserve to be frightened, humiliated, intimidated, physically, sexually, or emotionally hurt, controlled or coerced. Whether dinner was late, or you didn't anticipate something he thinks you should have, or you drank too much, or did something else about which you feel ashamed – you do not deserve to be abused, and you deserve to receive the support you need to be safe.

> *It is true that I was not the good mother I wanted to be. Too often, when my children were noisy and rambunctious, I lost control. I wanted to hold my temper, but I didn't. I would scream at them to stop. I would warn them to calm down. Sometimes I would hit them or shake them, or worse. I would throw things at them. I felt remorse afterwards and promised myself that I would never do it again, but the next day there would be a repeat of the battle.*
>
> *After lots of support and counseling and prayer, I came to understand that even when I did things I knew were terrible, it still didn't justify his abuse of me. I realized that I needed to take responsibility for my behavior and work on changing, but no matter what I did, I was not responsible for what he did.* [31]

Even strong women can be victims of abuse. It's not about how strong or knowledgeable you are, what a good parent or partner you are, or anything else about you. Sometimes you think, "I should have known. I should have seen this." It is not always possible to predict or know at the beginning of a relationship that someone may become abusive, as many abusers are charming at the beginning. In fact, it is not about *anything* you are doing or are not doing. What is happening to you is about your partner's issues. Nothing you do can change your partner's behavior. You only have the power to make your own choices, not theirs.

Naomi Tucker [32]

Stop blaming yourself...he is, or should be, a mature
adult who can control his impulses. Nothing "got into
him," it was there all the time, and it just became evident
under these circumstances. What can be justified in a
5-year old cannot be justified in a 25-year old.

Rabbi Abraham Twerski [33]

*My rabbi said to me, "You have one obligation and that is to preserve
your life."* [34]

Jewish tradition teaches that *pikuach nefesh* (saving a life), supersedes
almost all other obligations. As Rabbi Elliot Dorff explains, according to
the Talmud, "Avoiding danger is a stronger obligation than any
prohibition." [35] This means deciding what actions you do or don't take
based on safety first for yourself and your children.

Eternal One, help me think not only of what I cannot do, but of what I
can do.

*I cannot make John do anything. I can acknowledge what's happening
in our relationship. I can work to trust my instincts and observations
that know the glances, the tone of voice, the words, that feeling in the
pit of my stomach that sometimes precede an attack. I can leave a set
of keys to the car and the house with my sister in case I have to leave
quickly. I can create a safety plan for the kids and myself. I can put
some money in a private checking account under only my name. I
can pray. I can see if there is someone I can safely ask for help.*

If I am not for myself, who will be for me? If I am not
for others, what am I? And if not now, when?

Mishnah, Avot 1:14

*It took awhile for me to really believe that I have a right to close the
bathroom door. I have a right to think for myself.*

Today I took care of myself. I feel great and only a little guilty.

Trust yourself. Create the kind of self that you will be
happy to live with all your life. Make the most of
yourself by fanning the tiny, inner sparks of possibility
into flames of achievement.

Golda Meir[36]

5 You Are Not Alone

But, I feel so alone. There is no one to really talk to. No one will believe me. From the outside, we look just fine. When we're in public I smile and act like everything is okay. It isn't. I look in the mirror and weep at who I have become. I am afraid almost all the time. I am drowning in loneliness.

When

○ The actions or threats of an abuser isolate you from friends and family

○ Disbelief and silence keep others from recognizing there is a problem and from being supportive of you

○ Shame and fear make trusting anyone seem impossible, including yourself and God

Then

○ You are likely to feel disconnected from yourself, from others, and from sources of healing.

Without contact with others in similar situations, or those who understand the complexity and pain of being hurt and humiliated by someone you love, of course you will feel alone.

YOU ARE NOT THE ONLY ONE

For years, clients calling SHALVA, a Jewish domestic violence agency in Chicago, would say, "Well, I guess I'm your first client. I feel embarrassed." The myth that abuse doesn't happen in the Jewish community and the denial that abuse happens to people like "us," forms a backdrop that silences victims and survivors. And, yet, there are at least 60 Jewish domestic violence agencies in the United States alone.

Domestic violence is the most common crime in the United States. According to the National Institute of Justice and Centers for Disease Control, National Violence Against Women Survey, 1998: A woman is battered by an intimate partner every 15 seconds in the United States. The incidence of domestic violence in gay and lesbian couples approximates that of heterosexual couples. [37] You are not the only one.

CONNECTING TO OTHERS

Victims and survivors of abuse often find compassion, help and comfort through participation in a support group.

I joined a domestic abuse support group. Who were these other women? How could I trust them? Initially, aside from my therapist, I did not tell anyone – not family, not friends – that I was going to a support group, let alone that I had contacted a Jewish agency that specialized in domestic abuse.

For months, I held onto that weekly support group like the lifeline it was. Each of those women held a piece of me. In the beginning I felt it was the only safe place where I could just be me and talk about the things that really concerned me, preoccupied me and scared me. I no longer felt isolated. No matter how Kafkaesque the process of change felt, no matter how distant I felt from those around me as I went through the motions of suburban-stay-at-home-carpool mom, I had my group. For months I spoke with some of the women in my group daily. Sometimes more than once a day. When I felt overwhelmed, I called my counselor and again resonated in my own body, feeling more like myself.

> *In group I experienced the healing of hearing others disclose...the healing of disclosing...of speaking out in spite of the fear. I experienced the wondrous healing that came from TELLING.*
>
> *I will never forget the feel of one woman's hand tightly gripping mine, telling me without words that she was not going to let go, as I trembled, fighting to let the words come out, to make sound. In those moments, many things fell into place. I looked around and knew that I was no longer alone with my nightmares. I saw the tears, the compassion and sorrow for me and the pain I'd suffered in the faces of everyone there. I have goose bumps even now, so many years later, as I remember that moment.*
>
> *They did not see me as damaged but as courageous and wonderful. They loved my humor, my creativity, my kindness and wisdom. They loved me. How healing. How wonderful. What a triumph! I had other individual friends who knew my story. This group thing was somehow different. I continue to be grateful for this experience, this group I found through coincidence. Someone once said coincidence is God's way of remaining anonymous.* [38]

And sometimes, there is joy!

Barbara Siegel, clinical director at a Jewish domestic violence agency, commented on a group at her agency, "The way these women support each other is amazing. They meet even during the weeks we don't officially meet. One day someone brought in a tape of the song 'I Will Survive.' The next thing I knew, everyone was on their feet dancing – frum, nonreligious, Reform, EVERYBODY!" [39]

The joy of this moment is reminiscent of the time after the Israelites escaped from the pursuing Egyptians:

> ...then Miriam the prophetess, Aaron's sister, took a timbrel in her hand, and all the women went out after her in dance with timbrels.
>
> *Exodus 15:20-21*

CONNECTING TO THOSE YOU KNOW

Nothing can replace talking with other survivors – people who have walked in your shoes. The commonalities and compassion that come from having faced danger offer something unique when participating in a domestic violence survivor support group.

At the same time, kindness and support from good friends, family and neighbors can also be an important resource. When possible, reach out to others for companionship and assistance. The chapter, "On Telling," explores the importance of discerning who you think is safe to tell about the violence in your relationship. Spend some time thinking about what kinds of concrete support would be helpful in your situation, and who might be able to offer it. Asking for something specific gives friends and family an opportunity to support you.

Sometimes it is not possible to make contact with others. Even then, remembering friendships can be a source of sustenance. It can remind you of your capacity for connection and of the possibility of places of rest and comfort.

CONNECTING TO NATURE

During times of tumult and pain, of healing and recovery, connecting to the earth, to any natural beauty around you or even in your memory, can nourish your soul and calm your body.

For some, connecting to the wonders of nature strengthens their connection to God, to the presence of what is good around them.

The best remedy for those who are afraid, lonely, or unhappy is to go outside, somewhere where they can be quite alone with the heavens, nature and God. Because only then does one feel that all is as it should be and that God wishes to see people happy, amidst the beauty of nature. As long as this exists and it certainly always will, I know that then there will always be comfort for every sorrow...And I firmly believe that nature brings solace in all troubles.

Anne Frank[40]

Speak to the earth; it will teach you.

Job 12:8

It is good to make a habit out of looking at the sky.

Rebbe Nachman of Breslov [41]

CONNECTING TO YOURSELF

Being mistreated again and again by your partner makes it hard to see what is right with yourself. When you are afraid in an intimate relationship, when you are bombarded with judgments of all that your abuser says is wrong with you, it becomes self-preservation to disconnect from yourself and your feelings – to define yourself according to the image your batterer creates. If you were also abused as a child, negative messages about yourself may run deep, causing you to judge yourself harshly. It is possible to rediscover who you really are – to connect to the divine spark within you.

When "home" is not a safe place, survivors find ways to rediscover who they are and how to be there for themselves. We are told:

> Go forth (*lekh lekha*) from your land, from your
> community of birth, from your ancestral home…
> (Genesis 12:1). One teacher explains that the verse
> means "Go to yourself." Go back to your essence in
> order to find out what you are really made of.
>
> *Rabbi Lawrence S. Kushner and Rabbi Kerry M. Olitzky* [42]

Today some are bound, as were our ancestors enslaved in Egypt. Tomorrow may we be free, through loving connections and the grace of God.

For now, dear God, may I find ways to connect to supportive and loving people, to the wonders of the natural world, and to myself.

6 My World is Shaken - Where is God?

> *How did this happen? How did I get here? No one would believe this.*
> *I don't believe it. The words, the looks, throwing things, lying down*
> *at night next to my partner in terror. Sometimes a voice inside asks,*
> *"Why is this happening to me? Where is God?"*

How can you believe in a benevolent God when you have been violated?
How can you remain in relationship with God in the midst of suffering?
These are complex questions with which scholars and laypeople have
struggled over the centuries. There is no single model of how to respond
to suffering, and no single answer for everyone.

> The context, the situation, all that has occurred in a
> person's life, will influence the type of perception that
> the person will bring to God in a particular situation.
> *Rabbi David Hartman* [43]

One person living with domestic violence begins to question believing in
anything, including God, while another's belief in God may grow
stronger. Some "would find life unbearably chaotic if they could not
believe that suffering, tragedy, and death were part of God's plan for the
world." [44] Some bring their suffering directly to God.

My God, my God, why have you forsaken me, and are
far from my help and my cry?
O my God, I call by day and night, but You don't
answer; and there is no surcease for me.

Adapted from Psalm 22:2-3[45]

Believing and trusting can be hard when you have been threatened,
humiliated, attacked, controlled and/or coerced by your partner. God
may seem like someone who abandoned you, or a concept created to
control you. This chapter offers prayers and ideas that may be helpful
for maintaining or building a connection with God in the midst of struggle.

WHO OR WHAT IS GOD?

Judaism is open to many concepts of God.

Donna rejects the notion of a God that decides things about her life. She
believes in the healing power of nature and what she calls a divine
energy that brings comfort and hope.

Sarah says her relationship with God, which began during childhood,
has kept her sane throughout the nightmare of being abused by her
husband.

Linda's search for something to believe in began as her partner's abuse kept her isolated from friends and family.

Sue bows to the God within her.

Julie doesn't believe in any power or authority – benevolent or otherwise – that exists outside herself. She is sustained and comforted by an inner voice, by writing and by long walks.

Sandra finds the rhythms and rituals of Judaism sustain and nurture her. She lights Sabbath candles weekly.

Survivors of trauma – whether of domestic violence, concentration camps, child abuse, or prisoners of war – sometimes find they need to revise their religious beliefs and conception of God. The following was written after the Holocaust.

> We believe not in a God of strength but in a fragile light
> of the spirit that is always threatened by the power of
> night and that must always be fought for...
>
> We believe not in an omnipotent God who will transform
> the reality closing in around us, which is the given of our
> lives, but in a God who in a delicate voice calls us from
> within that reality to break through its hardness and
> create a resting place for the Divine Presence.
>
> *Rabbi Edward Feld* [46]

Sometimes, in response to trauma and tragedy, you may find yourself needing to reformulate your concept of God and your relationship to God.

We can no longer believe in a divine intervention that will come from the outside, but we must learn that we can let holiness enter, that we can make a space for the divine, that which is most deeply nourishing, that which sparks the soul of each of us. When we listen to the silent calling of God, impelling us to reach out and shatter the hard reality constructed by evil, to affirm the humanity of our neighbor – that is divine intervention.

Rabbi Edward Feld[47]

To survive, we are seeking the spiritual strength that allows us to go on, to learn to trust again, to believe in a God who will protect and nurture us. In my own recovery I had to reinvent God for myself so that I could awaken each day with a sense of purpose and joy. Healing does not occur in a moment.

Marcia Cohn Spiegel[48]

CREATING YOUR OWN BLESSING

Reciting a blessing allows us to open ourselves to God's presence in our lives. The act of blessing is one of turning to that which is beyond our ability to understand, and recognizing our limitations…blessing and prayer are the starting point of our own dialogue with the Creator. We must give ourselves permission to be personal in our prayers.

We start by remembering the traditional blessing formula (Blessed art Thou, Lord of the Universe, who has…) and think about what names we choose for God. We define for ourselves what God's power, qualities and attributes are. We state the act, event, or circumstances for which we want a blessing, and finally we reiterate God's ability to act in the world.

Consider using this model to create the blessings you need now:

1. (Naming God) Blessed are You, _____
2. (Quality and attribute) who_____
3. (Event) be with me as _____
4. (God's ability to act) Blessed are you who

_____

Marcia Cohn Spiegel [49]

When suffering or living in danger, of course what we want is to be safe, healed, whole, free of pain. Following are several images, words and prayers you may find helpful when feeling blocked, weary or scared. It's not that belief replaces taking action for your safety. But it may be that building your connection to God gives you greater strength, support, and hope to do what you need to do.

Here is an image that might help you feel less alone when you are suffering, when you ask, "Where is God?"

WHEN YOU ARE SUFFERING

The Midrash explains that all the years we were enslaved in Egypt G-d kept a brick close by and in view at all times to be a constant reminder of the pain of the Jewish people and of our suffering. We as slaves were compelled to do back-breaking work and produce the brick and so it was a symbol of our suffering.

The Talmud tells us that when we suffer, G-d suffers and when human beings cry, G-d cries too. A rabbi once told me that this idea of keeping a symbol of our suffering and our pain in front of G-d at all times was not only true for communal suffering but true for individual suffering, personal suffering, and family suffering as well. That G-d keeps an image or symbol in view at all times generating compassion and tears of suffering for us.

I was thinking about the families SHALVA[50] serves, the women and children, and what possible symbol could there be for their suffering in situations of abuse? I thought of broken dishes. Broken mirrors. And, I began to think about women's cosmetics. I asked my wife what it is called when a woman puts on something to hide a bruise. She said it's called "concealer." So I began to wonder about the image of G-d sitting with a bottle of concealer, sometimes called cover-up. G-d sits. G-d holds this bottle of concealer and G-d cries. G-d cries for the physical pain and the injury, the bruises, for the symbol of concealer. Not only because of physical pain but the emotional pain, the isolation, the hiding, the shame that person needs to be concealed, to cover up. Conceal not only the physical injury, but the very reality, the terror, the external bruises and the internal bruises, conceal fear, minute by minute, fear for children, what it means to live with someone who you can't trust. To conceal not only with concealer but with a smile. By saying everything is okay. "We're fine, thank G-d." "I'm okay. I walked into a door." "I slipped on the ice." "We had a hard day." "He has a temper but that's okay." "It's my fault." To say, "We're fine" when we're not. And so, I see the image of G-d with a bottle of concealer, with tears for our families.

Rabbi Dr. Jerry Lob[51]

WHEN YOU FEEL BLOCKED...

Anger, resentment and fear may understandably block any sense of connection to God. At those times you have many options, including expressing your deepest fears and hopes to God. Rabbi Naomi Levy shares that she prays because talking to God heals her.[52]

If you feel cut off from God, consider the following prayer:

> Dear God,
>
> Open the blocked passageways to you,
> the congealed places.
>
> Help us open the doors of trust that have been
> jammed with hurt and rejection.
>
> As you open the blossoms in spring,
> even as you open the heavens in storm,
>
> Open us to feel your great, awesome,
> wonderful presence.
>
> *Rabbi Sheila Peltz Weinberg* [53]

WHERE IS GOD IN ALL THE SUFFERING IN THE WORLD?

> "Where is the dwelling of God?"
> This is the question with which the Rabbi of Kotzk
> surprised many learned Jews who happened to be
> visiting him.
> They laughed at him: What a thing to ask! Is not the
> whole world full of God's glory?
> Then he answered his own question:
> "God dwells wherever people let God in." [54]

Sometimes you can't let God in, or don't know how, or don't want to, or can't feel that God is present. That's okay, too. Sometimes you can borrow other people's ideas, or images or beliefs. For example,

> My experience with God teaches me that God is a being or force like electricity. And we humans are wired for this "electricity." The spark of God is always within us at birth, but it is up to us to energize ourselves with God. It is up to us to fill ourselves up with God, by allowing the "current" of God to flow through the wires of our veins and nerves...
>
> Prayer and meditation are the plug that connects us to God. Prayer and meditation are invitations for God to fill us up with the divine presence, to work in us, to speak to us, and to become known to us.
>
> *Rabbi Douglas Goldhamer*[55]

For some, a simple, unselfish act, an act of kindness by another person, has been a reminder that

> God is at the center of life, at the very heart of existence. The encounter with God has the power to create a place where evil no longer has dominion. In the anticipation and memory of ordinary acts of nurture that are woven together in time, we create the carpet for the entry of God.
>
> *Rabbi Edward Feld*[56]

God is like sugar in a glass of water: I can't see it, but I know it's there because I can taste – and can add to – the sweetness.

Sophia Benjamin [57]

Where we are, God is; where God is, we are, because we are one, inseparable and indivisible.

Rabbi Douglas Goldhamer [58]

WHEN YOU FEEL WEARY…

I am weary and weeping all the time
For my body is crushed yet numb and
My heart aches
I hide nothing of my frightened heart, my failing
strength from You.
My friends distance themselves from the cause of my
pain; and my neighbors stand even farther away.
[My abuser] cleverly entraps me and tells lies all
the time.
It is as if I am deaf and cannot speak
I act as if I cannot hear or argue.
In you, God, do I hope. You will answer.

Based on Psalm 38:7-16 [59]

WHEN YOU FEEL SCARED...

> When I am afraid, I trust in You, in God, whose word
> I praise.
>
> *Psalm 56:4-5*

Turning to God in times of pain and suffering is part of our tradition. While trapped or isolated – literally or psychologically – many survivors maintain or establish a connection to God. Some say that since contact with God isn't traceable, it's safe.

Many who live with abuse talk to God about their pain, loneliness, hopes and fears. Some look to psalms or prayer for solace and strength. Prayer can be as simple as "help!" or "thanks!"

Some recite the following psalm to remember God's omnipresence.

> Where can I escape from Your spirit?
> Where can I flee from Your presence?
> If I ascend to heaven, You are there;
>   If I descend to Sheol, You are there too.
> If I take wing with the dawn
>   To come to rest on the western horizon
>   even there Your hand will be guiding me,
> Your right hand will be holding me fast.
>
> *Psalm 139:7-10*

Some complain to God.

> With my voice, I cry unto God; with my voice, I make
> supplication unto God.
> I pour out my complaint before God, I declare my
> trouble before God.
> When my spirit faints within me – God knows my path –
> in the way wherein I walk have they hidden a snare
> for me.
> Look on my right hand, and see, for there is no man that
> knows me;
> I have no way to flee; no man cares for my soul.
> I have cried unto You, God; I have said: "You are my
> refuge, my portion in the land of the living."
> Attend to my cry; for I am brought very low; deliver me
> from my persecutors; for they are too strong for me.
> Bring my soul out of prison, that I may give thanks unto
> Your name; the righteous shall crown themselves
> because of me; for You will deal bountifully with me.
>
> *Based on Psalm 142* [60]

Some talk to God even when they're not sure God exists. They invoke
God's presence.

> Evoke the Presence of God, whatever that may mean for
> you, and recite...psalms and prayers – slowly, being in
> God's Presence, and thinking about the words.
>
> *Rabbi David Blumenthal* [61]

Some prefer "talking" in their own words – written, spoken aloud, or to themselves. Questioning, beseeching, blaming, praising, discussing with God – Judaism supports all of these. Many survivors find solace engaging in dialogue with God, revisiting and refining their relationship to the Divine. These, too, are your right and your choice.

7 On Anger

Sometimes I get so angry I feel like I'm going to explode. This is sooooo unfair! Sometimes I want to hurt somebody. It's crazy. That isn't me. I don't really want to hurt anybody. Well, except sometimes. I'm just so furious, so scared and so FED UP!

Of course you get angry. That's normal. It's human. Even God, while slow to anger, gets angry and needs a time out to cool down. [62]

You may be angry at your abuser, at yourself, at the police for believing your partner rather than you, at your family or friends for not supporting you, at God for allowing this to happen or for neglecting you.

It may scare you when you get angry. You may fear that you'll become abusive with your children or your partner. Perhaps sometimes you have. You may feel like you're living in a pressure cooker and wonder how much longer you can keep the lid on.

There is a difference between getting angry and being abusive. Anger doesn't cause abuse. Everyone feels anger sometimes. Conflict within ourselves and with others is normal. Anger is physical energy that can be discharged safely in ways that don't hurt you or anyone else. Some survivors pound pillows (out of the presence of their children who might get scared seeing them so angry). Some write letters they never send, talk with friends, go to support groups, take a walk, knead bread or sing very, very loudly. Many use their anger as fuel to take the actions needed to increase their safety and/or to advocate for safety for others.

EXPRESSING ANGER

Job expressed his anger to God. Some rabbis in World War II Europe ran to the forests and screamed at God, "Where are you?" Sometimes, writes Rabbi David Blumenthal, we demand an answer, "God Whom I praise, do not be silent." [63] Rabbi Naomi Levy expresses belief in a God whose actions are a mystery, who answers our prayers not by preventing terrible things from happening but by being beside us and filling us with strength and hope and love through good and bad times. [64]

AND SO SOME PRAY:

> The lot You have bestowed upon me is a heavy one. I
> am angry. I want to know why: why the innocent must
> suffer, why life is so full of grief.
>
> *Rabbi Naomi Levy* [65]

Rabbi Blumenthal suggests we pray our anger – to bring it to God. Blumenthal reminds us of the recurring theme of anger in the Book of Psalms:

> …all kinds of anger: personal, national, political, and
> even anger toward God. In fact, the anger in the psalms
> is so strong that it often takes the form of rage. Rage
> expressed, not repressed. Rage prayed, excluded
> from the divine-human relationship. This is a mode of
> prayer that needs to be revitalized.

One cannot always be angry and full of rage, for anger does indeed distract and distort. It can disconnect us from life, as easily as it connects us to life. However, the proper prayer life includes moments of deep anger, as well as times of tranquility and serenity. It includes moments of rage, as well as times of reflection and meditation; moments of sadness, as well as times of joy and praise; moments of depression, as well as times of gratitude and exultation; "To dwell in the house of [God] forever" together with "For how long, oh [God], for how long shall the wicked rejoice;" "Every breath shall praise God" together with "Oh God, make them as tumbleweed, as straw before the wind." Psalms, precisely because they flow from the sheer variety of human life, contain the whole range of human emotions, feelings, and awarenesses – all of them brought before God, all of them incorporated into a full and vital prayer life. One simply alternates, bringing first this and then that feeling before God, turning first this and then that emotion into prayer.

Rabbi David Blumenthal [66]

Praise me, says God, and I will know that you love Me.
Condemn me, says God, and I will know that you love Me.
Praise me or condemn Me, and I will know that you love Me.
Sing out My graces, says God.
Raise your fist against Me and be angry, says God.
Sing out graces or express anger,
Anger is also a kind of praise, says God.

Excerpt adapted from Aaron Zeitlin [67]

Are you angry right now? Consider expressing your anger to God.

> Unleash the tears and anger
> As I offer them to You,
> As You take them for healings' sake,
> Someday transforming to peace and calm.
>
> *Debbie Perlman* [68]

8 Healing from Shame – Remember Who You Are

I feel so ashamed. I rarely look anyone in the eye anymore. "Selfish. Stupid. Lazy. It's your fault. You're going to wear that? Do that?" Words and actions that make me feel smaller and smaller. The other night we were at some friends' house for dinner. My husband looked at our hosts and said, "What a great meal, and such a beautiful home." Then, looking at me, he said, "Too bad you can't do this."

We each experience shame at some point in our life. We feel shame when we say or do something that goes against the integrity of who we are. We feel shamed when someone says we're bad, or stupid, or worthless and/or treats us as if we are. It is so very difficult to feel good about yourself when your partner, who promised to love and honor you, tells you you're worthless, a disappointment. Abusive words and actions trample the spirit. What can you do? Remember who you are.

Who are you? You are a human being created in the image of God.

In the Torah it is written:

> …on the day when God made humans, they were
> fashioned in the image of God.
>
> *Genesis 5:1*

And Elohim created humankind in the divine image, in the image of Elohim created it, male and female created them.

Genesis 1:27 [69]

We have a divine spark within us.

I do have a deep conviction that within every Jew there is a *neshama*, a divine soul which is pure and holy.

Rabbi Abraham Twerski [70]

I didn't feel pure or holy. I felt like a wreck. I was afraid he would convince people that I was crazy, a bad mother, lazy, incompetent, etc. There were times I believed it myself. His voice was in my head, broadcasting the propaganda 24 hours a day. I realized I could be a pawn in his chess game, or decide to fight for my life. I thought, "I hate conflict. I'm not a good negotiator. He's better at this, more calculating. I cannot take him on. I am afraid." I couldn't focus on much, but I knew what I had to do to survive and remain present for my children. I saw a therapist twice a week, telling myself that I was scandalously weak for doing so. I got help for my older kids. I went to a group weekly. Nightly hot baths. Daily journal writing. Weekly meditation. Prayer. Lots of prayer. Tons of reading. I took it day by day, sometimes hour by hour. I tentatively reached out for support and learned to cherish those people who responded lovingly.

According to the *Kabbalah*, at some point in the beginning of things, the Holy was broken up into countless sparks, which were scattered throughout the universe. There is a god spark in everyone and in everything.

Rachel Naomi Remen, M.D. [71]

From Genesis we learn that we are all created in the image of God.

What does that mean, to be created in the likeness of a divine being? It means that every human being contains a spark of the divine; that each of us is blessed and beautiful; that every soul is holy and worthy; that divine presence is not only above us but within each of us. It also means that each of us is a mirror for God's law and values, and we must each take it upon ourselves to reflect divine acts and *mitzvot* in our daily lives.

If you are my equal, and we were created equally, and you and I are both created in God's image...then to strike out against you is to violate the fundamental principles of *Bereshit*, of our beginnings. To strike you is to strike the image of God...and therefore to strike you is to sin against God.

Naomi Tucker [72]

Rabbi Yehoshua ben Levi said: "An entourage of angels always walks in front of people, with a messenger calling out. And what do they say? 'Make way for the image of the Holy One!'" Midrash (Deuteronomy Rabbah, Re'eh)

A common malaise which many of us suffer is feeling that we are insufficient or somehow unworthy. It undermines our spirit and our intent and, unfortunately, leads to distress. Judaism teaches that each person is a world unto him or herself. A Mishnah (Sanhedrin 4:5) expresses this idea by teaching that if we destroy one life it is as if we have destroyed an entire world. What would it take for us to feel our full worth and uniqueness?

Imagine, if we could actually hear God's angels proclaiming our approach with the words, "Here comes an Image of God." Many of us need such a forthright reminder of our relationship to the Divine. When we walk around with a low sense of self, we deny God's presence in our very being. It is as if we have erased the image of God that resides in our souls. Affirming our inestimable worth can help. When you question yourself, you can stand before a mirror and say, "I am created in the Image of God." If you feel shamed or disregarded, you can say, "I am created in the Image of God and no one can take this fact away from me."

Rabbi Kerry M. Olitzky and Rabbi Lori Forman[73]

So, imagine God's angels walking in front of you as you walk through your day, trumpeting your arrival as they proclaim, "Make way for the image of God."

Remember who you are.

9 On Telling

Jewish tradition holds language to be both powerful and holy...Words provide the basis for community, for they permit and allow for dialogue among people.

Rabbi David Ellenson [74]

You may long to talk with someone – to TELL, and yet, what if? What if your partner finds out you've told? What if the person you tell doesn't believe you, or minimizes how serious the situation is? What if she or he talks to your partner about the abuse?

Telling, when to tell, who to tell are complicated by safety concerns, threats of retaliation by your partner, past retaliatory abuse that occurred, confidentiality concerns and availability of resources. People living in danger need resources and a plan in place that takes into account the complexity of their individual situations. These need to be in place before they tell because telling, revealing the secret, frequently becomes a time of escalation of threats, coercion, stalking, acts of abuse towards the adult victim and/or children – whatever tactics the abusive partner feels are needed to regain control and dominance in the relationship.

Domestic violence advocates can help you think through your options, plan for safety, plan when and who to tell, and what steps to take. They can help you think through

> how your partner may react. Advocates often work with
> you, as well as trusted friends and family you identify.
>
> *Leigh Nachman Hofheimer* [75]

In addition to issues of safety, some people worry that to tell is wrong;
some fear they will be judged. Rabbis, friends or family sometimes say,
"Shhhh. Don't tell. It's a *shanda* (shame)." They interpret the tradition of
lashon hara, which reminds us not to gossip or slander anyone, to mean
that even when you're being abused by a partner, you should keep quiet.
How, then, is it possible to talk about what is happening to you, if to do
so means saying something awful about another? Isn't telling people
that you are or have been abused a *Hillul Hashem* (desecration of God)?

Rabbi Mark Dratch reminds us that telling about abuse is not a
desecration of God (*Hillul Hashem*) but an honoring of God (*Kiddush
Hashem*). [76]

Rabbi Elliot Dorff writes:

> ...*Hillul Hashem*, far from prompting us to try to hide the
> abuse that is going on among us, should motivate us
> instead to confront it and root it out.
>
> Two commands within Judaism are sometimes
> misinterpreted to prevent someone from either helping
> others to extricate themselves from abuse or making
> one's own way out of an abusive situation. One is the
> prohibition against "evil speech" (*lashon ha-ra*), and the
> other is the Jewish need to avoid shame (*boshet*).
>
> While it is important to avoid defamatory speech as

much as possible, there are some very clear exceptions to the prohibition.

...when failure to disclose abuse to the proper authorities will result in continued abuse, the victim and, for that matter, anyone who notices the abuse are obliged to reveal the facts...[N]otifying the authorities… is not only permissible, but mandatory when it is done in an effort to prevent harm to another.[77] As Maimonides wrote, Anyone who can save (someone's life) and does not do so transgresses "You shall not stand idly by the blood of your neighbor" (Leviticus 19:16).[78]

Abuse of spouses, elderly parents and children has reached the extent of a *meitzar ha-tzibbur* – a menace to the community as a whole.

These Jewish legal principles together mean that abused adults have a positive obligation to ignore the issues of defamation of the abuser since that is necessary to save their lives, and their duty to report an abuser in the context of saving their own lives is even greater than their responsibility to disclose abusers of others.[79]

Naomi Tucker, Executive Director of a Jewish domestic violence agency, points to the biblical commandment in Leviticus 19:16 – *al ta'amod al dam re'echa* – "do not stand idly by the blood of your neighbor."

> …[It] is only the second half of a sentence. The full quote contains another well-known Jewish ethic, which is the prohibition against *lashon hara*. The full sentence reads: "Thou shalt not be a gossipmonger among thy people; neither shalt thou stand idly by the blood of thy neighbor."

> The first part – a warning against gossip – is commonly thought of as the prohibition against *lashon hara*, or speaking evil of someone. So we are not supposed to spread gossip, speak cruelly of someone or defame someone's character in the community. But in the same sentence, it is juxtaposed with the commandment of not standing idly when someone is hurt. In other words, Judaism teaches us to hold life's paradoxes in balance. So, on the one hand, the Torah says that we should not gossip indiscriminately about one another, that we should not talk about others in ways that might bring them harm. But, in the same sentence the Torah tells us that we must make a big exception to this if someone is being hurt. In fact, we are <u>commanded</u> to do something. The Torah doesn't specify what we are to do…just that it is our moral and holy obligation to do something if our neighbor's blood is being shed. Because our greatest obligation, after all, is *pikuach nefesh* – to save a life. So if it actually would harm someone to remain silent, then our obligation is to speak out. Here we are being held to a standard of community accountability. We are collectively responsible for the well-being of our community. [80]

If possible, find someone you can trust and tell them what's going on. You pick the time and place. That is your right. Trust your instinct. It is also your right to tell *only* when it feels safe and you are ready. It is the responsibility of the community to make it safe for victims and survivors to come forward without blame or punishment and to hold the abuser accountable.

10 Healing Heart and Soul

Not to have had pain is not to have been human.

Yiddish proverb

Whether or not you are still in an abusive relationship, further healing may be needed. When someone you trust and love attacks your dignity and/or physical safety, repair is necessary.

There's a healing, *refuah*, that can take place.

Rabbi A. Tendler [81]

Many are my heart's distresses: let me know Your ways, Eternal One; teach me Your paths.

Psalm 25:4, 17 adapted by Rabbi Chaim Stern [82]

Grief is an emotion, not a disease. It is as natural as crying when hurt, eating when hungry, sleeping when weary. Grief is nature's way of healing a broken heart.

Rabbi Earl A. Grollman [83]

TOWARDS WHOLENESS – *TIKKUN HA'NEFESH* – HEALING AND PERFECTING OUR INDIVIDUAL SOULS

> There is no one among us whose body or soul is not permeated by cracks, some wide, some narrow, some deep, others shallow. At times, so many of us feel fragile, fractured, wanting only to gather up the shattered pieces. If only we could put them back together, to be smooth, unblemished once more. But, our journey is not back into the past, but forward, into a future where we transform our pieces into a whole that is both strong and weathered.
>
> *A Journey Towards Freedom: A Haggadah for Women*
> *Who Have Experienced Domestic Violence* [84]

> …[O]n some level, when we greet the difficult, painful parts of life with openness, we are embracing our essential humanity. In the words of the great Hasidic master, the Kotzker Rebbe, "There is nothing so whole as a broken heart."
>
> Perhaps it is when our hearts are broken that we have the potential to be the most spiritually open – to be more sensitive and mindful of the blessings in our lives, to be more empathetic to the suffering of others.
>
> *Rabbi Brant Rosen* [85]

You can rebuild yourself, your life, through acknowledging the broken pieces and mending them with God's help. There is nothing stronger than a broken heart which has mended.

God, You are my shepherd; I shall not want.
You guide me to lie down in green pastures; to walk by still waters.
You restore my soul.
You show me my right path for that is Your Nature
Even when I walk through the valley of the shadow of death, I am not afraid, for Your strength and comfort are with me.
You prepare a table before me in the presence of my enemies.
You anoint my head with oil; my cup overflows.
Surely goodness and mercy shall follow me all the days of my life; and I shall dwell in Your house forever.

Psalm 23 [86]

El na refa na lah.
Please God, heal her.

Numbers 12:13 [87]

In our tradition, there is a prayer for healing called the *Mishebeirach*, which is generally said, or sung, in support of those with physical illnesses. Let us ask that our hearts might be mended, that we might be more fully present to effect our own healing.

Adrienne Affleck [88]

Mi she-bei-rach a-vo-tei-nu
M'kor ha-b'ra-cha l'i-mo-tei-nu,
May the source of strength
Who blessed the ones before us,
Help us find the courage
To make our lives a blessing,
And let us say, Amen.

Mi she-bei-rach i-mo-tei-nu
M'kor ha-b'ra-cha l'a-vo-tei-nu,
Bless those in need of healing
With *r'fu-a sh'lei-ma,*
The renewal of body,
The renewal of spirit,
And let us say, Amen.

Debbie Friedman and Drorah Setel [89]

LIFE HAS TO BE ABOUT MORE THAN PAIN

In the times when there is no immediate danger, survivors find moments of joy and grace bolster them. It can seem incomprehensible to look for good when you're living with danger. And yet science supports what the Torah teaches, that focusing on feelings of gratitude, appreciation, compassion and love makes us feel better. The heart has its own nervous system, its own "brain," and focusing on feelings of gratitude, appreciation, compassion and love can improve our health and sense of well-being. [90]

This is different from denying or pretending that things are better than they are. To deny danger and risk in our lives does not fulfill our obligation to honor and preserve our lives. It is healthy, healing, to acknowledge the good in our lives. And, if you are in danger, do whatever you can to get to safety, to be safe.

Some people think, "Well, if you can laugh, it can't be *that* bad." They're wrong. Victims don't laugh or rejoice about being abused, but about the moments and experiences in life that are funny or heartening. You have the right to laugh.

> What soap is to the body, laughter is to the soul.
> *Yiddish Proverb*

Rabbi Douglas Goldhamer reminds us that to be joyous is part of our tradition and believes that there is a reason God wants us to rejoice. "It's another way of saying, 'Have faith in me. Trust me. I will make things work out.' … 'Don't lose faith. Don't give up hope. Rejoice, for I am here.'" [91]

> Blessed are You, O Ruling Spirit of the Universe, who releases the bound; who uplifts the fallen; who heals the sick; who makes peace where there is strife; who consoles the bereaved; who gives sight to the blind; who girds "Israel" (all of us who struggle) with strength; who guides each person's step, and makes firm the earth beneath our feet; who "restores the years that the locust has eaten" and brings us to the high road of humanity.
> *Adapted from liturgy* [92]

For those who see the Eternal, the sun will shine with healing on its wings.

Based on Malachi 3:20[93]

Thank You, God, for gifts unknown already on the way.

Healing takes time and patience, the patience of good friends and family, and it also takes some difficult communication. People want to help, but they often don't realize what you are wrestling with. One of the toughest challenges for me is dealing with good, kind, intelligent people who cannot see through the charming, smooth outer shell of my husband. He is still fooling people. But, I remember that I was also fooled, at close range, for many years.

My children and I are engaged in the fun part of healing, realizing that we are happy, healthy, and have the power in us to make a difference in our own lives and in the lives of others. We are beginning to learn about our potential and to live it. We have had dreams and seen them come true. We work with many community organizations involved in helping others, too. Even though we can't yet give a lot of dollars, we can and do give of ourselves, and we enjoy our ability to do so.

Our ability to confront and acknowledge our past has given us the clarity and will to make our lives normal and balanced. It took a lot of work, and we stumbled often but we always moved forward. The strong and gentle guidance I received from our local Jewish domestic abuse agency opened doors and cleared pathways for us. We only had to step through and begin to work.

11 On Forgiveness

People say, "let bygones be bygones." Not this I say to them. I must remember or else I will go back and the abuse will continue and I will be beaten down again. I don't know if I could get up again. I must remember and move forward. One Holocaust memorial I saw in Europe read, "Forgive and never, never, never forget." How do I ever do that?

WHAT IS FORGIVENESS? IS IT THE GOAL?

Forgiving does not mean condoning. It doesn't mean forgetting. It can mean letting go and moving on. It is not just a matter of "deciding" to forgive. Forgiving someone does not have to mean being in contact with that person. It isn't something you do "for" someone else.

> There are many divergent ideas about forgiveness, many of which are diametrically opposed. One of the most basic dichotomies is that forgiveness is something we work to achieve, and conversely, that forgiveness is a spiritual gift.
>
> *Laura Davis* [94]

There's this weird Hollywood idea that all relationships should have a happy ending – that everyone should forgive everyone in the final scene. But if a man burns down my house, I don't owe him forgiveness; he owes me a house. No one ever talks about what the person who perpetrated the crime owes. It's always the victim who owes forgiveness these days, and that's ridiculous.

Real forgiveness restores the moral fabric of a community and a family. It says, "We are all accountable to each other. We owe each other a certain kind of treatment, and when someone violates those standards, the damage needs to be repaired."

Richard Hoffman [95]

For healing and well-being, forgiveness is not always the goal. Forgiving is helpful for some. It's one option. Yet, as Rabbi Aron Tendler said in relation to domestic violence, "some things are unforgivable." [96] Ultimately, you must do what is right for you.

The victim of interpersonal violence such as incest, abandonment, or battering does not owe the perpetrator anything and does not need to meet the perpetrator halfway. Although we all make mistakes, people who have been on the receiving end of gross mistreatment are not required to cultivate humility in order to mend relationships with the people who have hurt them.

Laura Davis [97]

It is possible to move on without forgiving.

> Forgiveness and moving on are not necessarily joined.
> For me it was possible not to forgive and to move on. It
> has been 29 years since I left my abusive relationship. I
> still haven't forgiven. I have moved on.
>
> *Toby Myers* [98]

For some people, feeling their feelings, then forgiving, are necessary steps in letting go and moving on.

> Once you have experienced your anger – within
> whatever ability you have, let go of it and the resentment
> and bitterness. *Mehilla*, totally eradicating whatever the
> bad things are, only God can do this.
>
> *Fayge Siegal* [99]

For some, the abuser must complete *teshuvah* before forgiveness can even be considered. If considering forgiveness, ask yourself, "Has this person changed? Made amends?" Has s/he done *teshuvah*? "Do I feel safe with him/her now?" Apologizing and asking for forgiveness are very different from completing the process of *teshuvah*.

ABOUT *TESHUVAH*

Saying "I'm sorry" is not enough. It is the responsibility of those who abuse to do *teshuvah*. *Teshuvah* is a lengthy and multi-stepped process. Those who abuse must acknowledge the harm they have done and seek to make amends. The steps of *teshuvah* have been described as follows: [100]

- ❍ *hakarat ha'chet*, recognizing that one has done wrong and may still be doing wrong

- ❍ *azivat ha'chet*, deciding to change one's behaviors

- ❍ *vidui*, confessing out loud what one has done wrong, including feeling regret and remorse

- ❍ *hachlata le'atid*, imagining oneself in the future doing things differently. (It is only when we confront a similar situation and do things differently that we can say repentance is complete.)

An additional step in the *teshuvah* process is that of making amends. Making amends includes apologizing, asking those who have been harmed for forgiveness and publicly confessing one's mistakes. In some situations, restitution must also be made.

SHLEMUT, SHACHRER – WHEN YOU CAN'T FORGIVE

For some, forgiveness is not possible now and seems unlikely ever. How can you move on when you can't forgive?

> When we are struggling with flashbacks and nightmares and a variety of ailments brought on by the abuse, forgiving the offender may be far from our minds, or our ability. While we may not be able to forgive, we cannot continue to live with rage, fear and anger. Perhaps we need to find a word other than forgiveness in order to move forward. Judaism has the concept of *shlemut*, wholeness, personal integrity and peace. Seeking *shlemut* may help us find our way toward recovery. There is also the concept of *shachrer*, to be free of, to be independent from, in other words to move beyond. When victims achieve *shlemut*, they may find the power to leave the abuse behind and move to a condition of *shachrer* to become survivors, even thrivers.
>
> *Marcia Cohn Spiegel*[101]

IT'S YOUR CHOICE

> There is wisdom in giving each other the space to formulate our own beliefs, have our own experiences, and draw our own conclusions. Let those who believe in working toward forgiveness strive to achieve it. Let those who believe it arrives through serendipity wait for its appearance from within. Let those of us who find certain things unforgivable seek other paths to peace. And let us all find wholeness – *shlemut*.
>
> *Laura Davis*[102]

12 Prayers For Peace and Protection

I want to be safe. I grow weary of being so scared. Weary of having reason to be so scared.

To be able to feel afraid, to know when there is danger, is a valued instinct - a gift. And yet, being afraid all the time, worrying what might happen next, is exhausting. Being able to discern when you need to be alert – ready to flee or take a stand – and when you can let go of fear is important. And so some pray.

> Give me the good sense to be afraid when there is
> something to fear, so that I make ready, as well as I can,
> for whatever threatens. And give me courage to stand
> up with grace against the troubles I cannot keep from
> coming my way. And make me willing to learn from
> what hurts me instead of feeling sorry for myself.
>
> *Rabbi Chaim Stern* [103]

Sometimes your mind can't think and your body is tired. Rest.

RESTING IN THE ARMS OF GOD

I want to be held and rocked back into myself
held in Your lap
a gentle back and forth motion
gently
rocking
back and forth
back and forth and
back and forth
and back
and forth
rocking me back into myself
into awareness of how tired I am
how wound up
I allow myself to be cradled as a child safe in her
mother's arms
I sigh
My heart rate steadies and slows
A soft and subtle light filters through me
And I remember
The light of God is my soul
And so
I rest [104]

OSEH SHALOM

May the One who makes peace in the high places make
peace for us and for all Israel, and let us say Amen. [105]

My Light, my God,
This only do I ask,
Only this:
To live in Your house
All the days of my life.
Keep me safe in Your tent
When evil days come.
Hide me in the shelter of Your tent;
Set me safe upon a rock.
When I call, hear my voice;
Be gracious and answer.
My heart tells me to seek You,
To seek Your presence.
God my help,
Do not hide Your face,
Do not forsake me!
Teach me Your ways,
Lead me in Your paths,
And help me to hope in You,
Help me to be strong
And take heart,
Still to believe I shall see Your goodness
In the land of the living.

Psalm 27, Rabbi Chaim Stern [106]

I will give you peace in the land, and you will lie down,
and no one will make you afraid.

Leviticus 26:6 [107]

SHELTER ME

Help me, dear God,
To lie down at night in peace
And awaken me to life renewed.

It is not the darkness outside in the night sky that I fear
But the waiting space
of silence
inside this place
in which I dwell.
My house is not a shelter of peace.

Shelter me
With your *sukkat shalom*
Please
Shelter me.

Help me, dear God,
To lie down this night in peace
And lift me up to life renewed.

The shadow of your wings,
might they really replace
this valley of death where I've walked alone?
Oh, guard me as I journey
to an open place, a sacred space
Where I feel safe and whole – at home.

Shelter me
With your *sukkat shalom*
Please
Shelter me now
Shelter me
Please.

Rabbi Cindy G. Enger [108]

I lift my eyes up to the mountains:
From where does my help come?
My help is from The Unseen One,
The maker of the heavens and the earth.

Psalm 121:1-2 [109]

MI SHEBEIRACH FOR VICTIMS OF ABUSE
(See Appendix D for Hebrew text)

May God Who blessed our patriarchs, Abraham, Isaac
and Jacob, Moses, Aaron, David and Solomon, and our
matriarchs, Sarah, Rebecca, Rachel and Leah; Who hears
our cries that are caused by our oppressors and Who
knows our sorrows, bless, protect, strengthen and heal
our brothers and sisters, fellow Jews, men and women,
boys and girls, holy and pure souls, who are abused,
tormented and violated in body and soul by parents or
teachers, husbands or wives, neighbors, friends or
strangers. May God protect them from the treacherous
deeds and violent acts of their abusers, and from the
perverseness of their tongues. May the Holy One guard
those who cry out and save them from every distress and
misfortune, from every trouble and illness. We join as a
community to acknowledge and proclaim that a vile
deed has been done in Israel which ought not to be done.
May our God Who is close to the broken hearted and
Who saves those whose spirits are crushed, save them
and redeem them from their pursuers. May God make
known to them the ways of peace and lead them in paths
of justice. May there be peace in their homes and
tranquility in their families. May they dwell in security,

and may none make them afraid. And may the verse be
fulfilled for them, "You shall forget your misery, and
remember it like waters that pass away...And you shall
be secure, because there is hope; you shall look around
you, and you shall take your rest in safety" (Job 11:16, 18).
May the Merciful One who answers the broken hearted,
answer us. May the Merciful One who answers the
humble of spirit, answer us. Now, swiftly and soon, and
let us say, Amen.

Rabbi Mark Dratch [110]

Blessed One, guide us on our journey.

13 Choose Life

We are given choice between life and death,
good and evil – and we choose life – l'chaim.

Based on Deuteronomy 30:19 [111]

Survivors of domestic violence talk about the need for life to be about
more than pain. Many have found that expressing gratitude and
appreciation helps build hope. They suggest, "Bless life. Bless life and
express your rage and fear and loneliness. And, get help."

SH'MA: PERSONAL DECLARATION OF FAITH

Hear, O Israel –
The divine abounds everywhere
and dwells in everything;
the many are One.

Loving life
and its mysterious source
with all my heart
and all my spirit,
all my senses and strength,
I take upon myself
and into myself
these promises:
to care for the earth

and those who live upon it,
to pursue justice and peace,
to love kindness and compassion.
I will teach this to our children
throughout the passage of the day –
as I dwell in my home
and as I go on my journey,
from the time I rise
until I fall asleep.
And may my actions
be faithful to my words
that our children's children
may live to know:
Truth and kindness
have embraced,
peace and justice have kissed
and are one.

Marcia Falk [112]

I get up. I walk. I fall down. Meanwhile, I keep dancing.

Attributed to Hillel [113]

Without denying the pain of your situation, acknowledge what is not wrong. Ask yourself, "What beauty is there for me to see right now?"

Meditate on the goodness around you…

> Under the spreading tree of Your affection,
> I will sit and meditate
> On the goodnesses You have brought,
> Counting the happy moments like glistening beads
> Strung to adorn my days.
>
> Light the shadowed corners with gentle glow,
> To fill my being with peace.
>
> *Debbie Perlman* [114]

Modeh/Modah ani lefanecha…Thank you, God, for waking me up and giving me another day. [115]

Just to be is a blessing. Just to live is holy.

Rabbi Abraham Joshua Heschel [116]

Bonnie was never allowed to sing on *Shabbos*. Everyone else in the family could sing except her. Her husband told her she had a bad voice. On her first *Shabbos* with her children she talked with her counselor about how sad she was. She spoke about singing a couple of notes at home and her children saying, "You're not supposed to sing." She looked at them, sang a few more notes, then burst into song. Her spirits lifted. For so long she had been silenced. The next time she came in, she'd signed up for singing lessons. With a sweet smile she said, "My children no longer say, 'Sha' when I sing. They sing with me." [117]

It is said that God likes us when we pray and loves us when we sing.

Jewish proverb

I CHOOSE LIFE!

Now when I talk to other women like me I tell them, "Push through your fear. It becomes less and less each time. Commit to yourself as a worthy human being. Take control and responsibility for your life. Not doing so leaves a vacuum for someone else to do so and you won't much like the results. Hang on to the belief, even when it seems absolutely impossible, especially when it seems absolutely impossible, that you will get through this. You can not only survive; you can create a life for you and your children that is no longer based on survival, but rather on joy, love, health, and happiness." "I know," I tell them, "because I have been there, and with a lot of help I have done this."

14 In Closing

> There was a time when you were not a slave, remember
> that. You walked alone, full of laughter, you bathed
> bare-bellied. You say you have lost all recollection of it,
> remember…You say there are no words to describe this
> time, you say it does not exist. But remember. Make an
> effort to remember. Or failing that, invent.
>
> *Monique Wittig* [118]

Joan tells of a time of despair, of physical and emotional pain. She and a friend went for a walk by the beach. They sat quietly along the water's edge, watching the sunset, listening to the ebb and flow of the waves. Joan's friend turned to her and said, "You are like the sun. You brighten up so many of our lives. Thank you." An image came to Joan – rays of light, of love, shooting out from her heart to the sun, the water, the sky and to each of the people, places and things she loved. Remembering her friend's words to her, she felt each golden ray return – filling her heart, her soul, her body. She began to cry as she felt her heart fill with love. The problems in her life were not gone, but some of the isolation and despair were. She remembered she was not alone.

As you track the golden rays of love traveling from your heart, we hope you can also feel those that are coming to you.

TOGETHER WE CAN DO WHAT WE CANNOT DO ALONE

For decades, brave individuals have told and listened to stories of violence and healing, of life and death in our communities. For decades, people have worked to understand what contributes to violence in relationships, what helps prevent violence and what helps adults and children heal from the trauma of violence at home. They have battled silence, denial, threats and insufficient resources. They have helped write new laws, create new services and develop a language to talk about violence, battering, abuse. They held onto hope and possibilities in the midst of danger, death and disinterest. They worked alone and in partnership. They said, "Yes, it does happen here. We are NOT immune."

There are still people and places who disbelieve and deny. Yet more and more voices are joining together to say, "No more silence. No more violence. No more violence in our Jewish homes." Conferences addressing domestic violence in the Jewish community draw hundreds of Jewish women, men and teens from all over the world.

> They come in blue jeans and braided hair, black hats and sheitels and t-shirts that read "righteous babe" and "domestic violence isn't kosher." They come with infants in their arms and little books with photos of children and grandchildren. They come coifed and casual, survivor and healer (sometimes they are both). They walk unaided, with canes and in wheelchairs. The babble of languages and accents is beautiful. Everyone comes passionate for peace and safety, and with lots and lots of opinions. No one is shy. The cynicism that often taints our dialogue is surrounded and infiltrated by those who hold hope – who affirm that it is possible to

end violence – to end the violations against women and children. They begin to describe what a world without violence would look like. They speak of money and cooperation; of research that challenges our beliefs; of successes and stumbling; of the role of rabbis, cantors, teachers and each and every one of us. They share their experience, strength and hope through written and spoken word, poetry and theater, research, awareness-raising and in an abundance of inspiring programs for empowering boys and girls to be strong and peaceful.

The call to action continues. Where and how can we influence and empower ourselves and others to create a world where all of us are safe? Together we will find the way. [119]

As you walk your individual path, as you discover safety and community, know that many people are working together to promote healing and to end violence. Whether or not we ever meet, there are many of us walking with you. Know that wherever you are in your life, you are not alone.

May the day be near when all of us live in safety and in peace within our homes, our communities and the world. Shalom.

Appendix A: Creating a Safety Plan

Planning for safety means recognizing that regardless of apologies or promises to change, a partner or spouse who has abused you before is likely to do it again. As a human being created in the image of God, you deserve to be safe, and you have a responsibility to protect yourself and your children as best you can. Only your abuser is responsible for his or her actions.

What is a safety plan? A safety plan is a set of strategies and resources you can use to minimize abuse directed at you and your children. Safety plans are fluid, ongoing, multi-layered and guided by you. They can be useful whether or not you live with your abuser.

Living separately from someone abusive may not mean you are safe. Sometimes abuse escalates as you are planning to leave and/or after you have left. Your abuser may continue to try to contact you, use your children to have continued access to you, or threaten you if he suspects you are leaving the relationship. You are the expert in knowing the risks and consequences of your abuser's behavior. Achieving safety is a process and is different for each individual. Working with a domestic violence advocate and other supportive people can assist you in enhancing your safety with every decision you must make for yourself and your children.

Safety planning can be most effective when all parts of the community – police, courts, religious leaders, community agencies, therapists, etc. – support victims' decision-making in determining their safety. Individuals and agencies within a community can enhance the effectiveness of a safety plan by holding abusers accountable for their actions.

Resources in your community and domestic violence hotlines can help you develop a comprehensive safety plan that will best meet your individual situation. If you don't know what's available in your community, call the National Domestic Violence Hotline at 1-800-799-SAFE (7233) or TTY 1-800-787-3224. Some communities have Jewish domestic violence services. For a listing, see www.JWI.org. Other resources are listed here in Appendix C.

Reporting domestic violence incidents to the police may raise safety concerns; this option should be discussed with a domestic violence advocate (see "People and Places that Can Help"). There may be situations in which calling 911 is not the best option for you. For example, if the batterer works for a law enforcement agency or you have concerns about your legal status (i.e. immigrant or refugee status). A domestic violence advocate can help you figure out a strategy that fits your circumstances. Whether or not you choose to call the police, it may be helpful to document evidence of abuse (i.e., take pictures, gather witness statements, keep tape recordings) to be used in civil or criminal proceedings such as protection orders, custody or divorce hearings.

The following are just a few of the elements that are included in safety planning. Examples for people with disabilities or who are concerned about their legal status as an immigrant or refugee are included.

Please contact your local domestic violence agency to get help in creating a safety plan for yourself and your family.

DURING AN ARGUMENT, OR IF YOU FEEL TENSION BUILDING

○ Try to move away from rooms that have possible weapons, such as the kitchen and bathroom. Try to stay near an exit. Stay away from small spaces where the abuser can trap you. If possible, get to a room with a door or window to escape.

○ Get to a room with a phone to call for help; lock the abuser outside if you can. If appropriate, call 911 for help.

○ If possible, look for an exit and/or yell for help. Run to a neighbor or friend for help.

○ Ask others to call 911 during an incident. Memorize or keep with you the phone number of someone who has agreed to call the police if they hear any disturbances coming from your home.

○ If the abuser cannot be stopped, focus on staying alive and protecting yourself.

○ If a police officer comes, tell him/her what happened; get his/her name and badge number and report/incident number.

○ Get medical help if you are hurt.

○ Take pictures of bruises or injuries.

○ Call a domestic violence program (see "People and Places that Can Help"); ask them to help you make a safety plan.

○ If your abuser threatens to call the Bureau of Citizens Immigration Services (formerly INS), remember:
  • You do not have to tell anyone, including the police, about your legal status.
  • You have the right to ask for a lawyer.
  • Contact a local domestic violence agency. Advocates can help connect you with available legal services for documented and undocumented persons. Legal protections and public benefits are available to you and your children – learn your rights.

THINGS TO DO WHEN YOU ARE NOT IN IMMEDIATE DANGER

SECURE WEAPONS

○ If there are weapons in your household such as firearms –
lock them up!

PLAN SOME WAYS OUT

○ Know where there is a safe exit from your home. What window,
elevator, fire escape or stairwell could you use?

○ Know where you would go to be safe if you have to leave, even if
you don't really think you need to. See above list, "During an
argument or if you feel tension building."

IF MOVEMENT IS DIFFICULT DUE TO INJURY, ILLNESS OR DISABILITY

○ Practice how you will exit your home or how you will get to a
phone.

○ Routinely ask your personal assistant to help you get out of bed
early in the day. It is easier to respond to an emergency when you
are mobile and rested.

○ Increase your access to mobility aids whenever possible. For example,
keep your cane or walker close by or move to your wheelchair.
Think about alternate ways to be mobile if these are taken away.

○ Make sure that your vehicle and any adaptations are in working order.

○ If you call a transit company to pick you up, give them the address
of a place you regularly frequent as your destination, but which is
different from the place you really plan to go to. This will lessen
your abuser's suspicion and keep your destination private.

PLAN WAYS TO BE ABLE TO COMMUNICATE

❍ Always keep an extra cordless or cellular phone with you; tuck it by your side in your wheelchair, on a walker, or in a scooter basket.

❍ Program safety numbers into the speed dial of the phone.

❍ Memorize safe numbers, including the police, family, and a local domestic violence agency.

❍ If possible, discuss your situation with a trusted neighbor. Ask them to call 911 if they hear a disturbance. Pick a code word to use with them if you need the police.

PLAN AHEAD - PUT THINGS TOGETHER THAT YOU MAY NEED

❍ Always keep a purse and car keys ready in a safe place.

❍ Have change on hand to make emergency calls.

❍ You may want to keep a packed bag ready, including important things that you'd need if you had to leave quickly. Give it to a friend or relative you trust. Here are some things you may want to include:
  • Money, checkbook, passbook
  • Medications and/or prescriptions
  • Identification: driver's license, social security card, passport, public assistance ID, green card and/or work permit
  • Any court orders
  • Birth certificates – yours and your children's
  • Clothing
  • Lease, rental agreement, or house deed
  • Insurance papers
  • House and car keys
  • Jewelry/saleable objects
  • Address book
  • Divorce papers
  • School records
  • Toys

TEACH YOUR CHILDREN

○ To stay out of the middle of fights

○ How to get to safety (identify which neighbors or friends to call or go to)

○ To call 911 with your name and address

> **Remember that no one ever deserves to be abused. Remember that your safety and that of your children always come first.**

IN ADDITION TO THE ABOVE, IF YOU ARE PLANNING TO LEAVE YOUR SITUATION

○ Open a bank account in your own name at a different bank. Cancel any bank accounts or credit cards you share.

○ Think about who your best resources are if you need money or to find shelter.

○ Plan ahead for where you will go.

WHEN YOU OR THE ABUSER HAS LEFT

○ Contact a local domestic violence agency to connect with community resources; and discuss expectations of the legal system or other available services.

○ Keep your court orders with you at all times.

○ Give photocopies of your court orders to your children's school, your employer, your neighbors, as well as your local police department.

○ Change the locks on your doors. Install solid core doors with dead bolts. Install devices to secure your windows.

○ If possible, install adequate outside lighting. Trim back bushes and vegetation around residence.

○ Discuss safety plans with your children.

○ Inform your children's school about who has permission to pick up your children.

○ Tell your neighbors and landlord that your abuser no longer lives there and ask them to call the police if they see the abuser near your home. Show your neighbors a photo of the abuser and tell them about your Order of Protection.

○ Ask someone to screen your telephone calls at home and at work.

○ Decide if you need an unlisted phone number. If harassing calls persist, notify local law enforcement; keep a written log of harassing calls and any answering machine tapes of calls with the abuser's voice and messages. Consider getting Caller ID on your phone.

○ Have someone escort you to your car or walk with other people if possible.

○ Vary your routes to and from work and arrange for someone to escort you to your car, bus, or train.

○ If communication is necessary between you and your partner, meet in public places or have a third party make contact and relay messages.

○ Talk with people who can provide you with support on domestic violence issues.

○ Plan what to do in various situations if the abuser confronts you.

TELEPHONE SAFETY

○ When calling a hotline, domestic violence agency, advocate, or attorney, block caller ID.

○ After calling any of these resources, make another call so the number you just called cannot be determined.

○ Figure out a safe way for these resources to contact you. It may be safest for you to contact them. If you give them permission to call you at home, make sure they know to block caller ID and that they should never leave a message on voice mail or a machine. Consider making or receiving phone calls from a pay phone if you believe your abuser is tracking you.

○ If you use a TTY or pager, make sure to erase the call from the memory.

CELL PHONE SAFETY

If your abuser manages the cell phone you use, and/or has access to your cell number or account information, be aware that:

○ Itemized cell phone bills list all the numbers you've called. This makes it possible for your abuser to track where you've been and with whom.

○ Some cell phones provide "global positioning" information that allows someone to know exactly where you are if your cell phone is "on."
  • Get a cell phone whose number and information your partner cannot access.
  • Whether or not this is possible, turn your cell phone off on the way to domestic violence shelters, counseling services, or any place you do not want to be tracked or followed.

INTERNET SAFETY ALERT

Computer use can be monitored and is impossible to completely clear. If you are afraid your Internet and/or computer usage might be monitored, please use a safe computer like a library or friend's computer. Call your local hotline, and/or call the National Domestic Violence Hotline at 1-800-799-SAFE (7233) or TTY 1-800-787-3224 for additional information.

Using the Internet Safely

(Guidelines from the American Bar Association Commission on Domestic Violence: www.abanet.org/domviol/internet.html)

○ Use a computer at a local library, a friend's house, or at work.

○ Change your password often.

○ Do not pick obvious words or numbers as a password.

○ Realize that an abuser who has access to your e-mail account may be able to monitor incoming and outgoing mail or send viruses to destroy your system.

○ Harassing or threatening e-mails can be printed and used as evidence of abuse. Orders of Protection have added "electronic harassment" to protect against e-mail, cell phone, and pagers being used as forms of abuse.

JEWISH COMMUNITY AND SAFETY PLANNING

As you develop a safety plan, questions may arise regarding attending synagogue or community activities, for example:

○ What if you want to attend services or other community activities, but think your batterer will be there?

○ What if you want your children to attend religious school or other community activities, but worry your batterer will be there or will take the children without your knowledge?

○ What role can your rabbi and synagogue play in enforcing a protection order?

○ What can you expect from your rabbi and members of the Jewish community?

Rabbis can offer enormous strength and guidance in coping with domestic violence. And yet, just like the rest of the world, they fall along a continuum from those who are very knowledgeable and compassionate about domestic violence to those who are misinformed and/or who collude with batterers, to those who themselves abuse. There are rabbis who say, "Jews don't abuse!" Many others, throughout the various Movements, are actively involved in learning what is needed to help those who have been abused or are currently being abused and to prevent abuse in future generations.

If there is a Jewish domestic violence agency in your community, they may be able to help you find a supportive rabbi, and/or to help you discuss your situation with your current rabbi and connect you to local resources. Domestic violence advocates can also work with you and your rabbi to develop a safety plan within your community/congregation. This might include a safety plan for attending services, for being involved in other community activities, for your children to attend religious school, and for enforcing court orders.

How can you decide whether to seek help from a particular rabbi? Part of that is based on your intuition and knowledge of the rabbi. Most importantly, do you feel safe with the rabbi? Have you, or has someone you trust, spoken with the rabbi about important personal issues and found the rabbi helpful? Does the rabbi talk openly, from the pulpit and in the community, about the existence of abuse?

"Yes" answers to the following questions may give some sense that the rabbi and the congregation are aware of the problems of domestic violence and are working to address them. Has the rabbi delivered sermons on domestic violence, on the importance of respect in relationships, and on justice for victims? Is there information on domestic violence in the synagogue newsletter, posted in the library, bathrooms or other places the congregation gathers? Is abuse awareness information provided in premarital counseling sessions? Does the synagogue offer healing services for people who suffer from physical, sexual and/or emotional abuse?

A rabbi doesn't have to be an expert on domestic violence to be of great help. A rabbi who accepts and acknowledges that abuse happens and who is willing to hold abusers accountable for their actions can help you create a safety plan for being involved in congregational activities, connect you to resources, and help with your healing process. A rabbi who is open to listening and learning can be a tremendous blessing.

As many survivors will tell you, "Trust your instincts. Have a safety plan you review regularly. Ask for help. Stand up for your right to participate safely and fully in your community."

Appendix B: People and Places that Can Help

The support network in your community may include domestic violence agencies, mental health counseling services, statewide domestic violence crisis hotlines, and legal aid resources that offer resources, advocacy and assistance. This section describes the purpose and services of domestic violence agencies and a brief explanation of crime victims' compensation and batterers' intervention programs. Appendix C lists some national resources, agencies and websites.

Since the late 1970's, a movement to provide safe space and vitally needed support services to abused women and their children led to the establishment of domestic violence agencies throughout the United States. The services offered by domestic violence agencies today may include emergency shelter, transitional housing, individual counseling, child care, support groups, and systems advocacy (i.e. legal advocacy – helping women go to court and obtain protection orders; help with housing resources or unemployment).

Over time, domestic violence agencies are gaining expertise in providing services to lesbian, bisexual, gay and transgendered persons, ethnic and racially diverse communities, survivors with disabilities, immigrant and refugee populations, and to specific communities such as abused Jewish women (i.e., Jewish domestic violence programs that are staffed and designed to meet the unique and diverse needs of Jewish women).

While most crisis centers are set up to help abused women, they can provide individual advocacy services, help find emergency shelter and provide hotel/motel vouchers for men living in abusive relationships. More services are being developed to address the unique needs of diverse cultural and religious populations.

DOMESTIC VIOLENCE AGENCY SERVICES

Domestic violence agencies offer a range of services to help you sort out your options and begin to take control of your life. The underlying goal of domestic violence agency services is to *empower* you to gain safety, autonomy, and self-determination in your own life. To achieve this goal, programs operate on a peer support, self-help model which recognizes that clients are courageous and resourceful people in need of information and support when making decisions about their lives.

Staff at domestic violence agencies may include advocates, counselors and volunteers. Domestic violence agencies that receive state and federal funding are obligated to make reasonable efforts to provide services to victims with disabilities, victims who are deaf and hard of hearing and victims who have limited English proficiency. Most agencies offer access to spoken and sign language interpreters and coordinate their services with other agencies to work with as many victims as possible. While services may vary, most domestic violence agencies offer the following services:

VICTIM SAFETY AND CONFIDENTIALITY

Fundamental physical safety and confidentiality are among the most important benefits domestic violence agencies provide. Most agencies have a 24-hour confidential crisis line that is frequently the point of entry to emergency shelter (free) or transitional housing (free to low cost, ongoing housing) services.

Safety is the starting point, a necessary condition for healing and recovery. To ensure the safety of clients, most domestic violence agencies, shelters and transitional housing have confidential addresses which are not available to the general public or to other service providers. Additionally, without your explicit written permission, domestic violence agencies will NOT confirm to anyone that they are providing services or shelter/transitional housing to you.

BASIC SERVICES

Domestic violence agency services generally include: crisis counseling, weekly support groups, individual counseling, advocacy services, referrals, and safety planning. Advocates can help you sort out your options, whether you are thinking of leaving your abusive partner or not. Most agencies have 24-hour hotlines or phone access available during business hours for crisis counseling, referrals and information. In many programs, individual counseling is available for both you and your children.

ADVOCACY SERVICES

Advocates assist in ongoing safety planning; facilitate connection with community resources; explain paperwork; and provide help with financial assistance, unemployment services, immigration issues and housing agencies.

Advocacy services frequently include help with obtaining court orders for protection and other forms of relief. Advocates familiar with how to apply for court orders as well as the court practices in your community can accompany you to court and discuss with you the benefits and impact of legal remedies. They can help you find out what your rights are as a domestic violence victim. Advocates also work to hold systems accountable and often push for needed reforms that benefit all victims.

PEER SUPPORT AND EMPOWERMENT

Agency staff and shelters offer an environment of understanding and support. Sharing stories of abuse and problem-solving with others in abusive relationships can provide validation and connection.

CHILDREN'S SERVICES

Many agencies also provide services for the children of those who are being abused. Services may include cooperative child care, weekly support groups, counseling and referrals for medical and other social services. When necessary, agencies will also make arrangements with the local school system to ensure that the children are able to continue their education while living in residential programs (shelter or transitional housing).

HOW TO UTILIZE A DOMESTIC VIOLENCE AGENCY [120]

Abused people in need of emergency shelter should call the 24-hour national or statewide domestic violence hotline for immediate crisis counseling and referrals to local domestic violence agencies. National and statewide domestic violence hotlines have a TTY line (for those who are deaf or hard of hearing), as well as staff who speak several languages (or access to translation through a language bank line). (See Appendix C for national toll-free numbers).

Even when emergency shelter is not needed, calling a domestic violence agency can provide assistance in safety planning, connection with local resources, and help prioritizing options in your present situation and in the event of a future emergency.

CRIME VICTIM COMPENSATION PROGRAMS

All states have programs which reimburse victims of crimes for certain out-of-pocket expenses, including medical expenses, lost wages, and other financial needs considered reasonable. To be eligible, you must report the crime to the police and cooperate with the criminal justice system. Victim assistance programs in your community can give you compensation applications and additional information.

BATTERERS' INTERVENTION PROGRAMS

These programs can help abusers who take responsibility for their actions learn how to stop their abusive behavior. Participation in these programs may be voluntary or part of a court order. Some states have a certification process that a batterers' intervention program must complete to prove that they offer effective services. It is important to realize that abusers are the only ones who can change their violent behavior. Successfully completing a batterers' program is *no guarantee* that an abuser will stop abusing.

This information is meant to affirm that you are not alone, that there are many resources and individuals in the world who want you to be safe and who will work in partnership with you. See a partial list of resources in the next chapter.

Appendix C: National Hotlines, Agencies and Websites

For information about domestic violence services in your community, the following contacts may be helpful. Not every community has domestic violence services and even fewer have services specifically for Jewish people. Not every social service agency (Jewish or secular) is familiar with intimate partner violence. Ask whatever resource you contact what experience they've had working with people in situations like yours. Sometimes you'll need to get help from more than one resource, e.g., a domestic violence agency and/or a counseling agency, your rabbi, attorney and/or private therapist. Some cities have Jewish domestic violence agencies. For a list of Jewish resources, visit Jewish Women International's website (www.jewishwomen.org). For descriptions of types of services generally available, see Appendix B, "People and Places that Can Help."

The inclusion or exclusion of a resource here does not signify either endorsement or rejection. Please evaluate any resource you contact to see if it is right for your purposes. When calling these resources or contacting these websites, remember to keep safety in mind. Computer use can be monitored and is impossible to completely clear. If you think your Internet and/or computer usage might be monitored, please use a safe computer (perhaps at a library or friend's). Call your local hotline, and/or call the National Domestic Violence Hotline at 1-800-799-SAFE (7233) or TTY 1-800-787-3224 for additional information. (See telephone, cell phone, and internet safety guidelines, pages 102-103).

NATIONAL HOTLINES

National Domestic Violence Hotline
Phone: (800) 799-SAFE(7233) or 1-800-787-3224 V/TTY
Website: http://www.ndvh.org

Toll-free 24-hour hotline with a database of more than 4,000 shelters and service providers across the United States, Puerto Rico, Alaska, Hawaii and the U.S. Virgin Islands. Bilingual staff and a language line are available for every non-English speaking caller. Deaf or hearing impaired women can also find help at the Hotline by calling the TTY line.

National Hotline for Victims of Sexual Assault
Rape, Abuse, and Incest National Network (RAINN)
Toll-free 24-hour Hotline: 1-800-656-HOPE (4673)
E-mail: info@rainn.org
Website: http://www.rainn.org

National sexual assault hotline. Calls to the hotline are instantly computer-routed to the 24-hour rape crisis center nearest the caller. They can also help in finding specialized services: groups for male, elderly, teen or disabled survivors, programs for people under age 12, spouses or family members, adults molested as children or LGBT survivors, as well as services via TTY, in Spanish or other languages.

CHILD ABUSE HOTLINES/RESOURCES

Domestic violence agencies may be able to help with issues of child abuse directly or through coordination with another agency.

Check your local yellow pages for child protective services, and/or family service agencies that address child abuse and/or contact the resources below.

Childhelp USA®
National Child Abuse Hotline available 24 hours a day:
1-800-4-A-CHILD®
(1-800-422-4453)

Hotline dedicated to the prevention of child abuse in the United States, Canada, U.S. Virgin Islands, Puerto Rico, and Guam. Staffed with professional crisis counselors who utilize a database of thousands of resources. Assists children in the midst of abuse, troubled parents, individuals concerned that abuse is occurring, and others requesting child abuse information. Communication in 140 languages is available as is three-way conversation with the hotline counselor, the caller, and the nearest assistance.

For sexually assaulted children and adults:
RAINN
Toll-free 24-hour Hotline: 1-800-656-HOPE (4673)
(see earlier listing)

FOR TEENS

Love is Not Abuse
Liz Clairborne, Inc.
Website: http://www.loveisnotabuse.com

This interactive site provides facts, quizzes, discussion forums and resources for teens.

SafePlace Teen Site
Website: http://www.austin-safeplace.org
(Go to site index, click on "Teen dating violence and sexual assault")

This site is hosted by SafePlace in Austin, Texas, and provides information on dating and sexual violence, sexual harassment, and healthy relationships.

When Love Hurts
Domestic Violence and Incest Resource Center
Melbourne, Australia
Website: http://www.dvirc.org.au/whenlove

This site provides a complete guide for teens on love, respect and abuse in relationships.

Love Doesn't Have to Hurt Teens
American Psychological Association (APA)
Website: http://www.apa.org/pi/pii/teen/contents.html

Website is focused on teen dating and violence within relationships.
The site provides resources and information for the friend, family, abuser,
and victim.

You may also call the National Domestic Violence Hotline:
(800) 799-SAFE(7233) or 1-800-787-3224 V/TTY.
For information about teens and dating violence, visit their website:
http://www.ndvh.org and click on "Teens and Dating Violence"

FINDING SERVICES FOR JEWISH DOMESTIC VIOLENCE VICTIMS/SURVIVORS

Contact the national hotlines listed earlier. Tell them you're looking for an agency familiar with both domestic violence issues and Jewish clients. Jewish domestic violence agencies are not available in all areas. You may also contact the following organizations to ask for help in finding people with expertise working with domestic violence within a variety of organizations.

Agunah Advocacy Project
Phone: (212) 752-7133
Website: http://www.jofa.org

For assistance obtaining a Jewish divorce (*get*).

Jewish Women International (JWI)
2000 M Street, NW, Suite 720
Washington, DC 20036
Phone: (800) 343-2823
Fax: (202) 857-1380
E-mail: info@jwi.org
Website: http://www.jewishwomen.org

Jewish domestic violence agencies as well as information on obtaining a *get* (Jewish divorce) can be found on their website. For national, international, state by state, immigration, *agunot* and teen resources directory go to http://www.jewishwomen.org/directory/index.htm

Shalom Task Force

Phone: (888) 883-2323

Hotline providing information on rabbinic, legal and counseling services for anyone in the Jewish community in an abusive situation.

RESOURCES OUTSIDE THE UNITED STATES

International Domestic Violence Crisis Line for abused American women in foreign countries

Phone: 866-USWOMEN (866-879-6636)

L. O. Combat Violence Against Women

Women's Aid Center
P.O.B. 5941 Herzlia
Israel
Website: http://www.no2violence.co.il

Shelters for abused women and their children. Hotlines for women in Hebrew and Russian. Hotline for children. Trains hotline volunteers. All lines are operated 24 hours a day.
Toll-free hot-line: 1-800-353-300
Hot-line for women in distress: 09-9505720
Hot-line for children and youth in distress: 09-9518927

RESOURCES INVOLVED IN ADVOCACY AND VIOLENCE PREVENTION

FaithTrust Institute
(previously known as Center for the Prevention of
Sexual and Domestic Violence)
Jewish Program
2400 N 45th Street #10, Seattle, WA 98103
Phone: 206-634-1903
Fax: 206-634-0115 (24 hours)
E-mail: info@faithtrustinstitute.org
Website: http://www.faithtrustinstitute.org

An inter-religious educational resource addressing issues of sexual and domestic violence. Their goal is to engage religious leaders in the task of ending abuse, and to prepare human services professionals to recognize and attend to the religious questions and issues that may arise in their work with women and children in crisis. Their emphasis is on education and prevention.

Family Violence Prevention Fund (FVPF)
Building One, Suite 200
1001 Potrero Avenue
San Francisco, California 94110
Phone: 415-821-4553 Fax: 415-824-3873
Website: http://endabuse.org/resources/facts
Domestic Violence Survival Kit: http://www.dvguide.com/content.html

FVPF's website provides information and links to resources. FVPF provides a clearinghouse on domestic violence education, prevention and public policy reform. The organization works to end domestic violence and help women and children whose lives are devastated by abuse.

Minnesota Center Against Violence and Abuse (MINCAVA)
School of Social Work
University of Minnesota, 105 Peters Hall
1404 Gortner Avenue
St. Paul, Minnesota 55108-6142 USA
Phone: 612-624-0721
Fax: 612-625-4288
Toll free in Minnesota: (800) 646-2282
Website: http://www.mincava.umn.edu/center.asp

Supports research, education, and access to information related to violence. Bibliography of *Sources on Sexual and Domestic Violence in the Jewish Community* by Marcia Cohn Spiegel, is available here.

National Clearinghouse for the Defense of Battered Women
125 S. 9th Street, Suite 302
Philadelphia, PA 19107
Phone: (215) 351-0010
Fax: (215) 351-0779

The Clearinghouse helps battered women who, faced with life-threatening violence from their abusers, are forced to defend themselves. Provides technical assistance, support, resources, networking and training nationwide.

National Coalition of Anti-Violence Programs
240 West 35th Street
Suite 200
New York, NY 10001
Phone: (212) 714-1184
Fax: (212) 714-2627
Website: http://www.ncavp.org

A coalition of over 20 lesbian, gay, bisexual, and transgender victim advocacy and documentation programs located throughout the United States. NCAVP documents and advocates for victims of anti-LGBT and anti-HIV/AIDS violence/harassment, domestic violence, sexual assault, police misconduct and other forms of victimization. It addresses the pervasive problems of violence committed against and within the lesbian, gay, bisexual, transgender (LGBT) and HIV-affected communities.

The National Council of Jewish Women (NCJW) Inc.
53 West 23rd Street
New York, NY 10010
Phone: (212) 645-4048
Website: http://www.ncjw.org

NCJW is a volunteer organization, inspired by Jewish values, that works through a program of research, education, advocacy and community service to improve the quality of life for women, children and families and strives to ensure individual rights and freedoms for all. StoP (Strategies to Prevent) Domestic Violence is a multi-pronged national initiative incorporating education, community action, advocacy and training to curtail violence in the home.

Appendix D: Hebrew Text of *Mi Shebeirach* for Victims of Abuse

מי שברך for Victims of Abuse

Rabbi Mark Dratch

מִי שֶׁבֵּרַךְ אֲבוֹתֵנוּ אַבְרָהָם יִצְחָק וְיַעֲקֹב מֹשֶׁה אַהֲרֹן דָוִד וּשְׁלֹמֹה וְאִמוֹתֵנוּ שָׂרָה רִבְקָה רָחֵל וְלֵאָה, הַשׁוֹמֵעַ צַעֲקָתֵנוּ מִפְּנֵי נוֹגְשֵׂינוּ וְהַיוֹדֵעַ אֶת מַכְאוֹבֵינוּ, הוּא יְבָרֵךְ יִשְׁמֹר, יְחַזֵּק וִירַפֵּא אֶת אַחֵינוּ וְאַחֲיוֹתֵנוּ בְּנֵי יִשְׂרָאֵל, אֲנָשִׁים וְנָשִׁים, יְלָדִים וִילָדוֹת, נְשָׁמוֹת קְדוֹשׁוֹת וּטְהוֹרוֹת, הַמוּכִּים הַמְעוּנִים וְהַנִּפְגָעִים בַּגוּף וּבַנֶּפֶשׁ עַל יְדֵי הוֹרִים אוֹ מוֹרִים, בְּעָלִים אוֹ נָשִׁים, שְׁכֵנִים, קְרוֹבִים אוֹ זָרִים, בְּמַעֲשֵׂי אָוֶן וּפוֹעַל חָמָס בְּכַפֵּיהֶם, וּבְרָמִיָה בִּלְשׁוֹנָם. הַקָדוֹשׁ בָּרוּךְ הוּא יִשְׁמְרֵם וְיַצִילֵם מִכָּל צָרָה וְצוּקָה וּמִכָּל נֶגַע וּמַחֲלָה כִּי נְבָלָה נֶעֶשְׂתָה בְּיִשְׂרָאֵל וְכֵן לֹא יֵעָשֶׂה. הַקָרוֹב לְנִשְׁבְּרֵי לֵב וְהַמוֹשִׁיעַ דַּכְּאֵי רוּחַ, יוֹשִׁיעֵם וְיִפְדֵּם מֵרוֹדְפֵיהֶם אֲשֶׁר מַחְשְׁבוֹתֵיהֶם מַחְשְׁבוֹת אָוֶן וְרוּחַ טוּמְאָה תְּכַסֵּם, יוֹדִיעֵם דֶּרֶךְ שָׁלוֹם וְיַדְרִיכֵם בְּמַעֲגְּלֵי צֶדֶק. יְהִי שָׁלוֹם בְּבֵיתָם שַׁלְוָה בְּמִשְׁפְּחֹתָם, יֵשְׁבוּ לָבֶטַח וְאֵין מַחֲרִיד. וִיקוּיַים בָּהֶם הַכָּתוּב, "כִּי אַתָּה עֲמָל תִּשְׁכָּח כְּמַיִם עָבְרוּ תִזְכֹּר... וּבָטַחְתָּ כִּי יֵשׁ תִּקְוָה וְחָפַרְתָּ לָבֶטַח תִּשְׁכָּב:" רַחֲמָנָא דְּעָנֵי לִתְבִירֵי לִיבָּא, עֲנֵינַן; רַחֲמָנָא דְּעָנֵי לְמַכִּיכֵי רוּחָא, עֲנֵינַן. רַחֲמָנָא רְחֵם עֲלָן, הַשְׁתָּא בַּעֲגָלָא וּבִזְמַן קָרִיב, וְנֹאמַר אָמֵן.

Notes

I INTRODUCTION

[1] Bureau of Justice Statistics Crime Data Brief, *Intimate Partner Violence, 1993-2001*, February 2003. Family Violence Prevention Fund Website: http://endabuse.org/resources/facts/

[2] *JPS Hebrew-English TANAKH* (2nd edition) (Philadelphia: The Jewish Publication Society, 1999). Unless otherwise noted, all English translations of Biblical texts are from this 1999 translation by The Jewish Publication Society.

[3] For further discussion, see Naomi Graetz, *Silence Is Deadly: Judaism Confronts Wifebeating* (Northvale, N.J.: Jason Aronson, 1998); Elliot Dorff, "Aspects of Judaism and Family Violence," in *Embracing Justice: A Resource Guide for Rabbis on Domestic Abuse* (ed. Diane Gardsbane; Washington, D.C.: Jewish Women International, 2002); and Elliot Dorff, *Love Your Neighbor and Yourself: A Jewish Approach to Modern Personal Ethics* (Philadelphia: Jewish Publication Society, 2003).

[4] Simkha Y. Weintraub, *Eighteen Jewish Spiritual Resources to Strengthen Our Spirits*. [cited March 2003/Adar 5763]. Online: http://www.jbfcs.org.home/18resources.html

2 HOW DO I KNOW IF I'M BEING ABUSED?

[5] Alana Bowman, Keynote address at SHALVA Unity luncheon, Chicago, Il., 14 March 1995. Attorney Bowman is the former supervisor of Los Angeles County's domestic violence prosecution unit and sat on the National Council on Violence Against Women.

[6] Unless otherwise noted, words of abuse survivors are direct quotes or adaptations from one of the following: clients or friends of author, or clients of Jewish domestic violence agencies. Identifying information has been changed to protect each individual's privacy.

[7] Under the Marriage Fraud Act of 1986, men (who are typically the legal permanent resident) are considered to be the sponsors of their wives, thus having control over a woman's ability to remain in the United States. See S. D. Dasgupta, "Women's Realities: Defining Violence against Women by Immigration, Race, and Class," in *Issues in Intimate Violence* (ed. R. K. Bergen; Thousand Oaks, Ca: Sage, 1998).

[8] Gavin de Becker, *The Gift of Fear and Other Survival Skills that Protect Us from Violence* (New York: Dell, 1997), 27-47, 83-88 and 231-253.

[9] Judith Lewis Herman, M.D., *Trauma and Recovery: The Aftermath of Violence – from Domestic Abuse to Political Terror*. (New York: Basic Books, 1992), 76-83.

[10] *To Save a Life: Ending Domestic Violence in Jewish Families*, prod. Jean Anton, writ. and dir. Maria Gargiulo, 35 min., FaithTrust Institute, 1997, videocassette.

3 WHAT JUDAISM SAYS ABOUT ABUSE

[11] Julie R. Spitzer, "Reform Sermon," in *Resource Guide for Rabbis on Domestic Violence* (ed. Diane Gardsbane; Washington, DC: Jewish Women International, 1996), 45.

[12] Abraham Twerski, M.D., *The Shame Borne in Silence: Spouse Abuse in the Jewish Community*, (Pittsburgh: Mirkov Publications, Inc., 1997), 70.

[13] Sherry Berliner Dimarsky, in Toby Landesman, "Hope Lives When We Listen and Talk," *SHALVA News* (Spring 1997): 1. Sherry Berliner Dimarsky served as executive director of SHALVA, a Jewish domestic violence agency in Chicago, Illinois, during its first decade of operation.

14 Dorff, *Love Your Neighbor and Yourself*, 156. Rabbi Eliezer quotation is from Mishnah Avot 2:10.

15 In Aviva Richman, "Local Activists Hit Orthodox Feminist Conference," *Baltimore Jewish Times*, 20 February 2004.

16 Naomi Tucker, sermon, May 2, 2003. Naomi Tucker is Co-Founder and Executive Director of Shalom Bayit (a Jewish domestic violence agency), San Francisco, California.

17 Spitzer, "Reform Sermon," 45-47.

18 *To Save A Life*, videocassette.

19 Tucker, sermon, May 2, 2003.

20 For an in-depth discussion of domestic violence and Jewish law, see e.g., Graetz, *Silence Is Deadly*.

21 Abraham Joshua Heschel, *Man's Quest for God: Studies in Prayer and Symbolism* (Santa Fe, N.M.: Aurora Press, 1998), 124.

22 Rachel Lev, *Shine the Light: Sexual Abuse and Healing in the Jewish Community* (Boston: Northeastern University Press, 2003), 46.

23 Dorff, *Love Your Neighbor and Yourself*, 178.

24 Translation by Rabbi Cindy G. Enger.

25 Naomi Tucker, excerpt from essay written for Shalom Bayit, 1997. By permission of author.

26 Seek justice: Deuteronomy 16:20. Love your neighbor: Leviticus 19:18.

27 From the Kavannah in *The Policy Guidelines on the Prevention of and Response to Abuse* (July, 2002), Kehilla Community Synagogue. Guidelines available at http://www.kehillasynagogue.org/

28 In Lev, *Shine the Light*, 163.

29 Julie R. Spitzer, *When Love is Not Enough: Spousal Abuse in Rabbinic and Contemporary Judaism* (New York: The National Federation of Temple Sisterhoods, 1991), 51.

4 WHY IS THIS HAPPENING TO ME?

30. Judith Glass, "Afterbirth," in *Lifecycles: Jewish Women on Biblical Themes in Contemporary Life* (vol. 2; eds. Debra Orenstein and Jane Rachel Litman; Woodstock, Vt.: Jewish Lights Publishing, 1994), 187.

31. Adapted from Masha Gladys, "A Mother's Story" in Lev, *Shine the Light*, 98.

32. Naomi Tucker, personal communication, April 2004.

33. Twerski, *The Shame Borne in Silence*, 24-5.

34. *To Save a Life*, videocassette.

35. Elliot Dorff, "Jewish Law and Tradition," in Lev, *Shine the Light*, 55.

36. Source unknown.

5 YOU ARE NOT ALONE

37. "Based on our limited information, researchers have detected several similarities between battering experiences of lesbians and heterosexual women.... There are important differences." *Sourcebook on Violence Against Women* (eds. C. M. Renzetti, J. L. Edleson, Raquel Kennedy Bergen; Thousand Oaks, Ca.: Sage Publications, Inc., 2001), 167. According to Anne-Marie Ambert, Ph.D., the rate of violence among same-sex couples approximates that of heterosexuals, between 12 and 33 percent, depending on the sample and measures (Murray A. Straus and Richard J. Gelles, *Physical Violence in American Families: Risk Factors and Adaptations to Violence in 8,145 Families* (New Somerset, N.J.: Transaction Publishers, 1989). Online: http://www.arts.yorku.ca/soci/ambert/publications/extracts/families_11.html

38. Lev, *Shine the Light*, 109.

39. Barbara Siegel, M.S., LCPC is clinical director of SHALVA and a recipient of the State of Illinois 2004 Woman to Woman: Making a Difference Award.

40 Anne Frank, *The Diary of a Young Girl* (New York: Pocket Books, 1958), 143.

41 *The Sayings of Rebbe Nachman of Breslov.*
Online: http://home.global.co.za/~baalshem/prayer.htm

42 Lawrence S. Kushner and Kerry M. Olitzky, *Sparks Beneath the Surface: A Spiritual Commentary on the Torah* (Northvale, N.J.: Jason Aronson, 1993), 16.

6 MY WORLD IS SHAKEN – WHERE IS GOD?

43 David Hartman, "Suffering," in *Contemporary Jewish Religious Thought – Original Essays on Critical Concepts, Movements, and Beliefs* (eds. Arthur Allen Cohen and Paul R. Mendes-Flohr; New York: Scribner, 1987), 945.

44 Hartman, "Suffering," in *Contemporary Jewish Religious Thought*, 945.

45 Adapted from Psalm 22:2-3 by author.

46 Edward Feld, *The Spirit of Renewal: Finding Faith after the Holocaust* (Woodstock, Vt.: Jewish Lights Publishing, 1991), 143.

47 Feld, *The Spirit of Renewal*, 141.

48 Marcia Cohn Spiegel, "Spirituality for Survival: Jewish Women Healing Themselves," *Journal of Feminist Studies in Religion* 12 (Fall 1996): 124.

49 Marcia Cohn Spiegel, "Creating Your Own Blessing," in *TRADITIONS – The Complete Book of Prayers, Rituals, and Blessings for Every Jewish Home* (eds. Sara Shendelman and Dr. Avram Davis; New York: Hyperion, 1998), 176-181.

50 SHALVA is a domestic violence agency which serves the Jewish community in Chicago, Illinois.

[51] This was part of Rabbi Dr. Lob's remarks upon receiving the Glady Iser Award from SHALVA in 2003 for his service and activism on behalf of safety in Jewish lives in Chicago. Lob is a clinical psychologist in private practice.

[52] Naomi Levy, *Talking to God – Personal Prayers for Times of Joy, Sadness, Struggle, and Celebration* (New York: Doubleday, 2003), 14-15.

[53] Sheila Peltz Weinberg in *Kol Haneshamah: Shabbat Vehagim/Shabbat Eve* (Elkins Park, Pa.: Reconstructionist Press, 1989), 96.

[54] This is a story of the Kotzker Rabbi adapted by Martin Buber (which appears at the end of the *Shabbat Vehagim Kol Haneshamah* prayer book in a meditation for the month of Elul). Also in Martin Buber and Martin S. Jaffee, *Hasidism and Modern Man* (Philadelphia: University of Pennsylvania Press, 1988), 175-76.

[55] Douglas Goldhamer and Melinda Stengel, *This Is for Everyone: Universal Principles of Healing Prayer and the Jewish Mystics* (Burdett, N.Y.: Larson Publications, 1999), 44.

[56] Feld, *The Spirit of Renewal*, 142.

[57] Sophia Benjamin, "God and Abuse: A Survivor's Story," in *Four Centuries of Jewish Women's Spirituality: A Sourcebook* (eds. E. M. Umansky and D. Ashton; Boston: Beacon Press, 1992), 334.

[58] Goldhamer and Stengel, *This Is for Everyone*, 43.

[59] Adapted from Psalm 38:7-16 by author.

[60] Adapted from Psalm 142 by author.

[61] David Blumenthal, "A Spiritual Guide for the Jewish Patient," in *Voices in Our Midst: Spiritual Resources* (ed. G. R. Gary; Atlanta: Scholars Press), 37-40.
http://www.emory.edu/COLLEGE/JewishStudies/BLUMENTHAL/JewishPatient.html#fn1

7 ON ANGER

[62] Adapted from Exodus; See Exodus 32:9-14; 34:6-7. For more on God becoming angry, see Psalm 7:12 and Babylon Talmud, Brachot 7a. The author thanks Rabbi Avi Weinstein for suggesting Brachot 7a as an example.

[63] From Psalm 109, in David R. Blumenthal, *Facing the Abusing God* (Louisville, Ky.: Westminster/John Knox Press, 1993), 124.

[64] Levy, *Talking to God*, 159.

[65] Levy, *Talking to God*, 161.

[66] David R. Blumenthal, "Liturgies of Anger," *Cross Currents* (Summer 2002), Vol. 52, No. 2, 178 - 99.

[67] Source unknown.

[68] Debbie Perlman, *Flames to Heaven: New Psalms for Healing and Praise* (Wilmette, Il.: RadPublishers, 1998), 184.

8 HEALING FROM SHAME – REMEMBER WHO YOU ARE

[69] Author's interpretation of Genesis 5:1 and Genesis 1:27.

[70] Twerski, *The Shame Borne in Silence*, 54.

[71] Rachel Naomi Remen, M.D., *My Grandfather's Blessings: Stories of Strength, Refuge, and Belonging* (New York: Riverwood Books, 2000), 2.

[72] Excerpt from essay written by Naomi Tucker for Shalom Bayit, 1997. By permission of author.

[73] Kerry M. Olitzky and Lori Forman, *Sacred Intentions: Daily Inspiration to Strengthen the Spirit, Based on Jewish Wisdom* (Woodstock, Vt.: Jewish Lights Publishing, 1999), 311-12.

[74] David Ellenson, "Preface," in Rachel Adler, *Engendering Judaism – An Inclusive Theology and Ethics* (Boston: Beacon Press, 1998), viii.

[75] Leigh Nachman Hofheimer, personal communication, May, 2004. Leigh Nachman Hofheimer is Program Coordinator at the Washington State Coalition Against Domestic Violence and a member of FaithTrust Institute's Jewish Advisory Committee.

[76] *To Save A Life*, videocassette.

Notes 77 through 78 are citations from quoted material by Rabbi Elliot Dorff in, "Jewish Law and Tradition Regarding Sexual Abuse" in Lev, *Shine the Light*, 250.

[77] B. *Bava Kamma* 56a; S.A. *Hoshen Mishpat* 28:1, gloss. In B. *Pesahim* 113b, Rav Papa has a man named Zigud punished for testifying alone against another man named Tuvya on the ground that the testimony of a single witness is inadmissible and so Zigud, knowing that he was the only witness, was effectively spreading defamatory information (*motzi shem ra*) about Tuvya. That, however, was when the act had already occurred; the requirement in *Bava Kamma* and in the comment of Isserles to testify even singly in all cases in which there is a benefit, including preventing another person from sinning, refers to a future gain.

[78] Mishnah Torah *Laws of Murder* 1:14. In 1:15, Maimonides adds both affirmative and negative injunctions to this obligation based on Deuteronomy 25:12, "And you shall cut off her hand [being applied here to the abuser]; your eye shall have no pity." See also Rashi, B. *Sanhedrin* 73a, s.v. *lo ta'amod*.

[79] Dorff, "Jewish Law and Tradition Regarding Sexual Abuse" in Lev, *Shine the Light*, 55.

[80] Tucker, sermon, 2003.

[81] *To Save a Life,* videocassette.

[82] Chaim Stern, *Day by Day – Reflections on the Themes of the Torah from Literature, Philosophy, and Religious Thought* (New York: Central Conference of American Rabbis Press, 1998), 182.

[83] Earl Grollman, "How to Talk to Kids about Death," *Jewish News of Greater Phoenix*, Jewish Family & Life (June 13, 2003/Sivan 13 5763) 55.

[84] Allison Iser et al., *A Journey Towards Freedom: A Haggadah for Women Who Have Experienced Domestic Violence*, (Seattle: FaithTrust Institute, 2003), 8.

[85] Rabbi Brant Rosen, "There is Nothing So Whole as a Broken Heart," sermon for Erev Yom Kippur, 5764. Rabbi Brant Rosen is rabbi of Jewish Reconstructionist Congregation, Evanston, IL. Used with permission.

[86] Author's interpretation of Psalm 23.

[87] Translation by author.

[88] Adrienne Affleck, "Sukkoth of Healing from Domestic Violence," in Lev, *Shine the Light*, 219.

[89] Lyrics by Debbie Friedman and Drorah Setel, music by Debbie Friedman. *Mi Shebeirach* from *And You Shall Be a Blessing* (Sounds Write Productions, Inc., ASCAP, 1988).

[90] Doc Childre and Howard Martin with Donna Beech, *The HeartMath® Solution: The Institute of HeartMath's Revolutionary Program for Engaging the Power of the Heart's Intelligence* (San Francisco: HarperCollins, 1999).

[91] Goldhamer and Stengel, *This Is for Everyone*, 64-65.

[92] Adapted by Wendy Rabinowitz from the daily morning liturgy. See: *The Prayer Book: Weekday, Sabbath and Festival* (Ben Zin Bokser, ed.,

New York: Hebrew Publishing Company, 1957), 38-9; *Siddur Sim Shalom* (Rabbi Jules Harlow, ed., New York: The Rabbinical Assembly, The United Synagogue of America, 1985), 11; *The Artscroll Siddur*, (New York: Mesorah Publications, 1969), 19.

93 Author's interpretation based on Malachi 3:20.

11 ON FORGIVENESS

94 Laura Davis, *I Thought We'd Never Speak Again – The Road from Estrangement to Reconciliation* (New York: HarperCollins, 2002), 266. This book offers helpful insight into the ways in which forgiveness may or may not play a role in the healing process, especially Chapter 9, "The Question of Forgiveness," 265-292. Workbook to this text available online: www.lauradavis.net

95 Richard Hoffman in Davis, *I Thought We'd Never Speak Again*, 269.

96 *To Save a Life*, videocassette.

97 Davis, *I Thought We'd Never Speak Again*, 254.

98 Personal communication with author, 2004. Toby Myers, a longtime worker in the Texas Battered Women's Movement, maintains a limited private practice, works with attorneys in domestic violence cases (usually as an expert witness), and trains in the area of domestic violence. She is a member of FaithTrust Institute's Jewish Advisory Committee.

99 Fayge Siegal, personal communication, March, 2004. Fayge Siegal is a founding mother and current board member of SHALVA, Chicago's Jewish domestic violence agency.

100 Rabbi Moses Ben Maimon, known as Maimonides, codified the process of *teshuvah* in the twelfth-century. The description of the process here is based on Estelle Frankel, *Sacred Therapy: Jewish Spiritual Teachings on Emotional Healing and Inner Wholeness*, (Boston: Shambhala Publications, Inc. 2003), 143-148.

[101] Marcia Cohn Spiegel, "Forgiveness and the Jewish High Holy Days," in *Forgiveness and Abuse: Jewish and Christian Reflections* (eds. Marie M. Fortune and Joretta Marshall, Binghamton, NY: The Haworth Press, Inc., 2002), 26.

[102] Davis, *I Thought We'd Never Speak Again*, 292.

12 PRAYERS FOR PEACE AND PROTECTION

[103] Stern, *Day by Day*, 251.

[104] Toby Landesman, © 1997, used with permission.

[105] From the liturgy.

[106] Stern, *Day by Day*, 187-8.

[107] Translation as found in Iser, *A Journey Towards Freedom*, 47. One may also translate *v'ayn makhareed* as "and no one will terrify you."

[108] *Shelter Me* is an adaptation of *Hashkiveynu*, a prayer that is part of the liturgy for evening worship. *Hashkiveynu* is a petition to God for protection through the night and from its dangers, asking God to spread over us a *sukkat shalom*, a shelter of peace, that we might find refuge in the shadow of God's wings.

[109] *Kol Haneshama: Shabbat Vehagim* (Elkins Park, Pa.: Reconstructionist Press, 1989), 53-54.

[110] Used with permission of author.

13 CHOOSE LIFE

[111] Author's interpretation based on Deuteronomy 30:19.

[112] Marcia Falk, *The Book of Blessings: New Jewish Prayers for Daily Life, the Sabbath, and the New Moon Festival* (San Francisco: Harper, 1996; paperback edition, Boston: Beacon Press, 1999), 24-27.

[113] Attributed to Hillel. Source unknown.

[114] Perlman, *Flames to Heaven*, 11.

[115] Adapted from daily morning liturgy.

[116] Abraham Joshua Heschel, *The Wisdom of Heschel*, selected by Ruth Marcus Goodhill (New York: Farrar, Straus & Giroux, 1975), 220.

[117] Toby Landesman, "Will this be a sweet year?" *SHALVA News*, Autumn 2003.

14 IN CLOSING

[118] Monique Wittig, *Les Guerilleres* (New York: Viking Press, 1969), 89.

[119] Toby Landesman, adapted from "Pursuing Truth, Justice and Righteousness: A Call to ACTION Jewish Women International Conference 7/22/03." *SHALVA News*, Autumn 2003.

APPENDIX A: CREATING A SAFETY PLAN

[120] Adapted and excerpted from S. Martin, "Shelters For Battered Women and Their Children," in *Domestic Violence, A Training Curriculum for Law Enforcement, Volume II: Reference Materials* (San Francisco: The Family Violence Project, District Attorney's Office, 1990).

Selected Bibliography

DOMESTIC AND SEXUAL VIOLENCE IN THE JEWISH COMMUNITY

Antonelli, Judith S. *In the Image of God: A Feminist Commentary on the Torah*. Northvale, N.J.: Jason Aronson, 1995. [See sections on child abuse, incest, rape, wife abuse.]

Benjamin, Sophia. "God and Abuse: A Survivor Story." Pages 326–334 in *Four Centuries of Jewish Women's Spirituality: A Sourcebook*. Edited by Ellen M. Umansky and Dianne Ashton. Boston: Beacon, 1992.

Biale, Rachel. *Women and Jewish Law: An Exploration of Women's Issues in Halakhic Sources*. New York: Schocken, 1984.

Blumenthal, David R. *Facing the Abusing God: A Theology of Protest*. Louisville: Westminster/John Knox, 1993.

Carnay, Janet. *The Jewish Women's Awareness Guide: Connections for the 2nd Wave of Jewish Feminism*. New York: Biblio, 1992. [See chapters "Shalom Bayit," "Control of Our Bodies," "Taking Action," and "From Chance to Choice."]

Chalew, Gail Naron, ed. "Forum: Family Violence is a Jewish Issue." *Journal of Jewish Communal Service* 68, no. 2 (Winter 1991): 94–139.

Cwik, Marc Steven. "Peace in the Home? The Response of Rabbis to Wife Abuse within American Jewish Congregations." *Journal of Psychology and Judaism* 20, no. 4 (Winter 1996): 279–348; 21, no. 1 (Spring 1997): 5–81.

Dorff, Elliot N. *Love Your Neighbor and Yourself: A Jewish Approach to Modern Personal Ethics*. Philadelphia: Jewish Publication Society, 2003. [See especially chapter five.]

Dratch, Rabbi Mark S. "Forgiving the Unforgivable? Jewish Insights into Repentance and Forgiveness." *Journal of Religion and Abuse* 4, no. 4 (2002): 7–24.

Eilam, Esther. "Rape and Rape Survivors in Israel." Translated by Sharon Ne'eman. Pages 312–318 in *Calling the Equality Bluff: Women in Israel*. Athene Series. Edited by Barbara Swirksi and Marilyn P. Safir. New York: Pergamon, 1991.

Featherman, Joan. "Jews and Sexual Child Abuse." Pages 128-155 in *Sexual Abuse in Nine North American Cultures: Treatment and Prevention*. Edited by Lisa Aronson Fontes. Thousand Oaks, Calif.: Sage, 1995.

Gardsbane, Diane, ed. *Embracing Justice: A Resource Guide for Rabbis on Domestic Abuse*. Washington, DC: Jewish Women International, 2002.

——. *Healing and Wholeness: A Resource Guide on Domestic Violence in the Jewish Community*. Washington, DC: Jewish Women International, 2002.

Gargiulo, Maria. *Broken Vows: Religious Perspectives on Domestic Violence*. Videocassette [59 min.] and study guide. Seattle: FaithTrust Institute [formerly known as Center for the Prevention of Sexual & Domestic Violence], 1994.

——. *To Save a Life: Ending Domestic Violence in Jewish Families*. Videocassette [35 min.]. Seattle: FaithTrust Institute [formerly known as Center for the Prevention of Sexual & Domestic Violence], 1997.

Giller, Betsy. "All in the Family: Violence in the Jewish Home." Pages 101–109 in *Jewish Women in Therapy: Seen but Not Heard*. Edited by Rachel Josefowitz Siegel and Ellen Cole. New York: Harrington Park, 1991.

Gluck, B., "Jewish Men and Violence in the Home – Unlikely Companions?" Pages 162–173 in *A Mensch among Men: Explorations in Jewish Masculinity*. Edited by Harry Brod. Freedom, Calif.: Crossing, 1988.

Goldberg, Natalie. *The Great Failure. A Bartender, A Monk, and My Unlikely Path to Truth.* HarperSanFrancisco, 2004.

Graetz, Naomi. *Silence Is Deadly: Judaism Confronts Wifebeating.* Northvale, N.J.: Jason Aronson, 1998.

Green, Lilian. *Ordinary Wonders: Living Recovery from Sexual Abuse.* Toronto: Women's Press, 1992.

Greenberg, Yitzchak. "Rabbis Can Help by Speaking Out." *Moment*, April 1990, 49.

Gross, Netty C. "Machismo Gone Mad? 21 Israeli Women Murdered in 18 Months by the Men Who Loved Them." *Jerusalem Report.* Dec. 6, 1999, 20–25.

Jacobs, Lynn and Sherry Berliner Dimarsky. "Jewish Domestic Abuse: Realities and Responses." *Journal of Jewish Communal Service* 68, no. 2: (Winter 1991–2): 94–113.

Lev, Rachel. *Shine the Light: Sexual Abuse and Healing in the Jewish Community.* Boston: Northeastern University Press, 2003.

Matas, Carol. *The Primrose Path.* 1995. Reprint, Winnipeg: Blizzard, 1998.

Orenstein, Debra. "How Jewish Law Views Wife Beating." *Lilith 20* (Summer 1988): 9.

Russ, Ian, Sally Weber and Ellen Ledley. *Shalom Bayit: A Jewish Response to Child Abuse and Domestic Violence.* Los Angeles: Jewish Family Service of Los Angeles, Family Violence Project, 1993.

Scarf, Mimi. *Battered Jewish Wives: Case Studies in the Response to Rage.* Lewiston, N.Y.: Edwin Mellen, 1988.

Siegel, Rochelle. "Domestic Abuse and Jewish Women: Opening the Shutters." *Jewish Women's Journal* 2, no. 3 (Summer 1994): 17–19.

Silverman, Sue William. *Because I Remember Terror, Father, I Remember You.* Athens: University of Georgia Press, 1999.

Spiegel, Marcia Cohn. "The Last Taboo – Dare We Speak About Incest?" *Lilith 20* (Summer 1988): 10–12.

Spitzer, Rabbi Julie Ringold. *When Love is Not Enough: Spousal Abuse in Rabbinic and Contemporary Judaism.* New York: Women of Reform Judaism, The Federation of Temple Sisterhoods, 1995.

Swirski, Barbara. "Jews Don't Batter Their Wives: Another Myth Bites the Dust." Pages 319–327 in *Calling the Equality Bluff: Women in Israel.* Edited by Barbara Swirski and Marilyn P. Safir. New York: Pergamon, 1991.

Twerski, Rabbi Abraham. *The Shame Born in Silence: Spouse Abuse in the Jewish Community.* Pittsburgh: Mirkov, 1997.

Wisechild, Louise M. *The Obsidian Mirror: An Adult Healing from Incest.* Seattle: Seal, 1993.

GENERAL BOOKS ON DOMESTIC VIOLENCE, SEXUAL VIOLENCE, SAFETY, HEALING, AND PREVENTION

Bancroft, Lundy. *Why Does He Do That?: Inside the Minds of Angry and Controlling Men.* New York: Berkley, 2002.

Bancroft, Lundy and Jay G. Silverman. *The Batterer as Parent.* Thousand Oaks, Calif.: Sage, 2002.

Bass, Ellen and Laura Davis. *The Courage to Heal: A Guide for Women Survivors of Child Sexual Abuse.* New York: HarperPerennial, 1994.

Creighton, Alan and Paul Kivel. *Battered Women's Alternatives.* Oakland, Calif.: Oakland Men's Project, 1992.

——. *Helping Teens Stop Violence: A Practical Guide for Counselors, Educators, and Parents.* Alameda, Calif.: Hunter House, 1992.

Davies, Jill M., Eleanor Lyon and Diane Monti-Catania. *Safety Planning with Battered Women: Complex Lives/Difficult Choices*. Sage Series on Violence against Women 7. Thousand Oaks, Calif.: Sage, 1998.

Davis, Laura. *I Thought We'd Never Speak Again: The Road from Estrangement to Reconciliation*. New York: HarperCollins, 2002.

Engel, Beverly. *The Emotionally Abused Woman: Overcoming Destructive Patterns and Reclaiming Yourself*. New York: Ballantine, 1992.

Evans, Patricia. *The Verbally Abusive Relationship: How to Recognize It and How to Respond*. Holbrook, Mass.: Adams Media, 1996.

Gargiulo, Maria. *Love – All That and More: A Six-Session Curriculum and 3-Video Series on Healthy Relationships for Youth and Young Adults*. Videocassette [66 min.]. Seattle: FaithTrust Institute [formerly known as Center for the Prevention of Sexual & Domestic Violence], 2001.

Gottman, John Mordechai and Neil S. Jacobson. *When Men Batter Women: New Insights into Ending Abusive Relationships*. New York: Simon & Schuster, 1998.

Groves, Betsy McAlister. *Children Who See Too Much: Lessons from the Child Witness to Violence Project*. Boston: Beacon, 2002.

Herman, Judith Lewis. *Trauma and Recovery*. New York: BasicBooks, 1992.

Island, David and Patrick Letellier. *Men Who Beat the Men Who Love Them: Battered Gay Men & Domestic Violence*. New York: Harrington Park, 1991.

Jones, Ann. *Next Time She'll Be Dead: Battering & How To Stop It*. Boston: Beacon, 2000.

Jones, Ann and Susan Schechter. *When Love Goes Wrong: What to Do When You Can't Do Anything Right*. New York: HarperCollins, 1997.

Kivel, Paul. *Boys Will Be Men: Raising Our Sons for Courage, Caring, and Community*. Gabriola Island, B.C.: New Society, 1999.

Lew, Mike. *Victims No Longer: Men Recovering from Incest and Other Child Sexual Abuse*. New York: Nevraumont, 1988.

Lewis, Barbara A. *What Do You Stand For?: A Kid's Guide to Building Character*. Edited by Pamela Espeland. Minneapolis: Free Spirit, 1998.

Maltz, Wendy. *The Sexual Healing Journey: A Guide for Survivors of Sexual Abuse*. New York: Perennial Currents, 2001.

NiCarthy, Ginny. *Getting Free: You Can End Abuse and Take Back Your Life*. Seattle: Seal, 2004.

——. *The Ones Who Got Away: Women Who Left Abusive Partners*. Seattle: Seal, 1987.

NiCarthy, Ginny and Sue Davidson. *You Can Be Free: An Easy-to-Read Handbook for Abused Women*. 1989. Reprint, Seattle: Seal, 2000.

Renzetti, Claire M. *Violent Betrayal: Partner Abuse in Lesbian Relationships*. Newbury Park, Calif.: Sage, 1992.

SOURCES OF INSPIRATION AND SOLACE

This list includes sources for healing rituals.

Affleck, Adrienne. "Sukkoth of Healing from Domestic Violence." Pages 213–219 in *Shine the Light: Sexual Abuse and Healing in the Jewish Community* by Rachel Lev. Boston: Northeastern University Press, 2004.

Berner, Leila Gal. "Our Silent Seasons – A Ceremony of Healing from Sexual Abuse." Pages 121–136 in *Lifecycles: Jewish Women on Life Passages and Personal Milestones*. Lifecycles 1. Edited by Debra Orenstein. Woodstock, Vt.: Jewish Lights, 1994.

Cardin, Rabbi Nina Beth. *Out of the Depths I Call to You: A Book of Prayers for the Married Jewish Woman*. Northvale, N.J.: Jason Aronson, 1992.

Falk, Marcia. *The Book of Blessings: New Jewish Prayers for Daily Life, the Sabbath, and the New Moon Festival*. San Francisco: Harper, 1996; paperback edition, Boston: Beacon Press, 1999.

Goldhamer, Douglas Hirsch and Melinda Stengel. *This is for Everyone: Universal Principles of Healing Prayer and the Jewish Mystics*. Burdett, N.Y.: Larson, 1999.

Gottlieb, Lynn. "Recovering from the Violence in Our Lives: Mikveh and a Public Recovery Ceremony for Women." Page 218 in *She Who Dwells Within: A Feminist Vision of a Renewed Judaism* by Lynn Gottlieb. HarperSanFrancisco, 1995.

Hilsen-Bernard, Wendy. *A Woman's Place: The Compassionate Guide for Reclaiming Body, Mind, and Life*. Brookfield, Conn.: Still River Resources, 2001.

Iser, Allison et al. *A Journey Towards Freedom: A Haggadah for Women Who Have Experienced Domestic Violence*. Seattle: FaithTrust Institute [formerly known as Center for the Prevention of Sexual & Domestic Violence], 2003.

Josefowitz Siegel, Rachel and Ellen Cole, eds. *Celebrating the Lives of Jewish Women: Patterns in a Feminist Sampler*. Binghamton, N.Y.: Harrington Park, 1997.

Klem, Yonah. "No Ordinary Bath: The Use of the Mikvah in Healing from Incest." Pages 123–130 in *Jewish Women Speak Out: Expanding the Boundaries of Psychology*. Edited by Kayla Weiner and Arinna Moon. Seattle: Canopy, 1995.

Levy, Naomi. *Talking to God: Personal Prayers for Times of Joy, Sadness, Struggle, and Celebration*. 2002. Reprint, New York: Doubleday, 2003.

——. *To Begin Again: A Journey Toward Comfort, Strength, and Faith in Difficult Times*. New York: Ballantine, 1998.

Olitzky, Rabbi Kerry M. and Rabbi Lori Forman. *Sacred Intentions: Daily Inspiration to Strengthen the Spirit, Based on Jewish Wisdom.* Woodstock, Vt.: Jewish Lights, 1999.

Perlman, Debbie. *Flames to Heaven: New Psalms for Healing & Praise.* Wilmette, Ill.: Rad, 1998.

Remen, Rachel Naomi. *My Grandfather's Blessings: Stories of Strength, Refuge, and Belonging.* New York: Riverhead, 2000.

Ribner, Melinda. *New Age Judaism: Ancient Wisdom for the Modern World.* Deerfield Beach, Fla.: Simcha, 2000.

Ritualwell.org. The Ritualwell website provides resources for creating innovative, contemporary Jewish rituals. Includes rituals for healing from abuse, and guidelines for making your own ritual. See http://www.ritualwell.org/MakingRituals/index.html.

Rogow, Faith. "Healing Rituals for Abused Jewish Women: Healing Our Bodies, Healing Our Souls." Available at http://www.ritualwell.org/Rituals/ritual.html?docid=813. First published in *When Love is Not Enough: Spousal Abuse in Rabbinic and Contemporary Judaism* by Rabbi Julie Ringold Spitzer. New York: Women of Reform Judaism, The Federation of Temple Sisterhoods, 1991.

Schwartz, Rebecca and Naomi Tucker. "Sukkat Shalom: A Healing for Battered Women and Their Allies." 1996. Available at http://www.shalom-bayit.org/. From the "Events, Help, Programs, and More…" menu, select "Resources."

Shalom-bayit.org. "Passover Haggadah Insert for Battered Jewish Women (May Be Used following the Recitation of the Ten Plagues)." Available at http://www.shalom-bayit.org/. From the "Events, Help, Programs, and More…" menu, select "Resources."

——. "Shalom Bayit Chanukah Candlelighting: Honoring Battered Women and Their Children." Available at http://www.shalom-bayit.org/. From the "Events, Help, Programs, and More…" menu, select "Resources."

Siegel, Bernie. *Peace, Love and Healing: Bodymind Communication and the Path to Self-Healing: An Exploration*. 1989. Reprint, New York: HarperPerennial, 1990.

——. *Love, Medicine and Miracles: Lessons Learned about Self-Healing from a Surgeon's Experience with Exceptional Patients*. New York: HarperPerennial, 1990.

Spiegel, Marcia Cohn, "Spirituality for Survival: Jewish Women Healing Themselves." *Journal of Feminist Studies in Religion* 12, no. 2 (Fall 1996): 121–137.

Spiegel, Marcia Cohn and Deborah Lipton Kremsdorf, eds. *Women Speak to God: The Prayers and Poems of Jewish Women*. San Diego: Woman's Institute for Continuing Jewish Education, 1987.

Stern, Rabbi Chaim. *Day by Day: Reflections on the Themes of the Torah from Literature, Philosophy, and Religious Thought*. New York: Central Conference of American Rabbis, 1998.

Umansky, Ellen M. and Dianne Ashton, eds. *Four Centuries of Jewish Women's Spirituality: A Sourcebook*. Boston: Beacon, 1992. [Pages 321–325 describe a woman's use of a *mikveh* to heal after rape.]

Related Resources Available from FaithTrust Institute

To Save a Life: Ending Domestic Violence in Jewish Families

An essential resource for abused Jewish women, Jewish communal leaders, helping professionals, and all who seek to break the silence about domestic violence in Jewish families. 35-minute video with study guide.

"This video covers all the bases. It thoroughly explores all the aspects of family violence amid an illuminating and supportive discussion of Jewish perspectives on the issue."

RABBI ELLIOT DORFF
RECTOR AND PROFESSOR OF PHILOSOPHY
UNIVERSITY OF JUDAISM

ORDER NO. V-302 $79.00 (PLUS SHIPPING)

A Journey Towards Freedom: A Haggadah for Women Who Have Experienced Domestic Violence

A Journey Towards Freedom transforms the traditional Passover Seder into a special service that addresses the oppression and liberation of women journeying from abuse to safety. An ideal resource for community groups, domestic violence organizations, and as a supplement to any Passover haggadah.

ORDER NO. HGD $15.00 (PLUS SHIPPING)

Love – All That and More

An ideal resource for Jewish educators to teach healthy relationship skills to youth and young adults. Incorporates examples and teachings from the Jewish tradition regarding love, honor, respect and integrity. Package includes: 3 videos, an 8-session curriculum with texts from Torah, Talmud and modern sources, and handouts for participants.

I recommend this video series as an integral part of every post bar and bat mitzvah program across the country."

Rabbi Sue Levi Elwell, Ph.D.
Pennsylvania Regional Director
Union of American Hebrew
Congregations

ORDER NO. VS-400 $285.00 (PLUS SHIPPING)

Shine the Light: Sexual Abuse and Healing in the Jewish Community

BY RACHEL LEV

This is an extraordinary journey into the stories, minds and hearts of adult Jewish survivors of sexual abuse and incest. The author reveals Judaism to be rich in resources for healing as she explores Jewish law, tradition and rituals that include the thoughts of rabbis, community leaders and survivors.

ORDER NO. STL $26.95 (PLUS SHIPPING)

For information about these resources, and about training and consultation on issues of abuse in Jewish communities, contact FaithTrust Institute toll-free at (877) 860-2255 or visit our website at www.faithtrustinstitute.org

Order Form

For additional copies of *You Are Not Alone: Solace and Inspiration for Domestic Violence Survivors Based on Jewish Wisdom*

Name _____

Organization _____

Address _____

City _____ State/Prov _____ Zip/Postal Code _____

E-mail: _____

Phone: Home: (   ) _____

            Work: (   ) _____

Number of Copies _____ @ $18.00 per copy (Quantity discount available for 5 or more copies. Call toll free 877-860-2255 in U.S. or 206-634-0055 outside U.S.)	$ _____
Washington state residents, add 8.8% sales tax	$ _____

Shipping/Handling costs within North America:

1-2 copies	$ 4.00	$ _____
3-4 copies	$ 8.00	$ _____
5 + copies	Call	$ _____

Shipping outside North America
(Call, fax, or e-mail first to get charges) $ _____

TOTAL ENCLOSED $ _____

ORDERS MUST BE PREPAID. Make checks payable to FaithTrust Institute and enclose with this order form. See reverse side of this form for mailing address.

Mail to:

>FaithTrust Institute
>2400 N. 45th St., Suite 10
>Seattle, WA 98103
>(206) 634-1903   FAX (206) 634-0115

For credit card orders:
call toll free 877-860-2255 in U.S. or 206-634-0055 outside U.S.,
or go to: www.faithtrustinstitute.org

FaithTrust
INSTITUTE

Working together to end
sexual & domestic violence

About the Author

Toby Landesman is a writer, story gatherer, photographer and consultant who believes strongly in healing through creative expression. Toby received her Bachelor of Arts degree from the University of Illinois at Urbana and completed a Master's Degree in Social Work at Loyola University of Chicago. A psychotherapist with over 30 years of clinical experience working with trauma survivors, Toby has extensive knowledge in the areas of domestic violence and child sexual abuse.

Toby's commitment to advocating for peace in people's lives began in the 1980's, with efforts to raise awareness about domestic violence in Jewish communities through community performances with the group, Bitachon – Safety for Jewish Women. She was also actively involved with SHALVA, a Jewish domestic violence agency in Chicago, serving as newsletter editor, speaker, trainer, and president of their board of directors.

Toby uses creative expression through a variety of media, including art, storytelling, and community performance, to promote individual and community healing. She is a member of Chicago's Task Force on Domestic Abuse in the Jewish Community and serves on the Jewish Advisory Committee of FaithTrust Institute.

Toby's Jewish soul has been nurtured by many sources throughout her life, from the rhythm of prayer in her grandmother's shul and watching her aunts dance the *sherala* at family celebrations, to participating in a youth group as a teen and working side by side with the women of SHALVA for over ten years. Her exploration of Judaism continues to deepen through study, prayer and meditation.